GW00383838

THE
ZACK CHUG
Cookbook

Table Of
Contents

SMOOTHIES

MEAL PREPS

Firstly, thank you so much for purchasing my cookbook, I am eternally grateful. A lot of time and effort has gone into this and I really appreciate your patience which has allowed me to release it.

I started this page and journey with the aim to motivate and inspire, I have been blown away by the IMMENSE support and love from you. I want to make sure people can enjoy their fat loss journey and not have to experience and face the same problems I did when losing 20kg of fat.

The aim of this cookbook is to help you eat and live healthily without feeling any guilt when eating specific foods. This cookbook would not have been possible without you guys.

I hope you enjoy and please tag me in all your recipe creations, I cannot wait to see them !

BREAKFAST

PANCAKES

Calories	220	Carbs	14g	Protein	16g	Fat	11g

INGREDIENTS:

2 eggs

60g banana

Tsp. cinnamon for the pancake mixture (optional)

Frozen berries (microwave to form a berry compote) (OPTIONAL)

THE **ZACK CHUG** Cookbook

METHOD

· Blend all the ingredients together for a smooth pancake texture.

· Heat for 3 minutes on each side at medium heat in the pan.

· Optional to top the pancakes with berry compote.

Scan me !!

PANCAKES

Calories	265	**Carbs**	22g	**Protein**	40g	**Fat**	3g

INGREDIENTS

70g banana

125g egg whites

Scoop of vanilla powder

Tsp. of baking powder

OPTIONAL 30g frozen berries

THE ZACK CHUG Cookbook

METHOD

- Blend all of your ingredients together into a thick batter.

- Add equal servings of batter to the pan on medium heat for 3-4 mins on each side.

- Optional to microwave frozen berries to form a berry compote topping.

Scan me !!

PANCAKES

| **Calories** 290 | **Carbs** 24g | **Protein** 17g | **Fat** 14g |

INGREDIENTS

80g banana

2 whole eggs

Tsp. cinnamon

10g dark choc chips

METHOD

• Blend your banana, eggs, and cinnamon into a pancake batter.

• Add equal portions of the batter to a pan.

• Pan fry on medium heat for 3 mins on each side of the pancake.

• Add choc chips whilst pan frying.

Scan me !!

THE ZACK CHUG Cookbook

HIGH PROTEIN LOADED
PANCAKES

Calories	395	Carbs	25g	Protein	53g	Fat	8g

INGREDIENTS

100g egg whites

90g of banana

1 scoop of protein powder

Tsp. of baking powder

Cooked turkey rasher

1 egg

Low calorie syrup

THE ZACK CHUG Cookbook

METHOD

- Before you make your pancakes, pan fry one turkey rasher and scramble one egg.

- For the pancake batter, blend your egg whites, banana, protein powder, baking powder into a thick pancake batter.

- For each pancake you can make from the batter, pan fry on medium heat for 3 minutes on each side of the pancake.

- Load it with your turkey rasher and scrambled egg.

Scan me !!

FRENCH TOAST

Calories	600	Carbs	99g	Protein	50g	Fat	8g

INGREDIENTS

2 oreos

75ml unsweetened almond milk

75g egg whites

1 scoop of chocolate protein powder

4 slices of low cal bread

5g of nutella

OPTIONAL low cal choc. sauce & oreo crumbs

METHOD

· Firstly crush 2 oreos.

· Add them to almond milk, egg whites and protein powder.

· Mix it all together and coat 1 slice of bread and then add nutella in the middle of it.

· Then add another slice of bread on top of the original slice and coat it again.

· Pan fry on low heat for 5 mins on each side.

· Repeat these instructions for another 2 slices of bread optional to top it off with choc sauce and oreo crumbs.

THE **ZACK CHUG** Cookbook

Scan me !!

Chug

HIGH PROTEIN
CREPES

| Calories | 250 | Carbs | 19g | Protein | 39g | Fat | 3g |

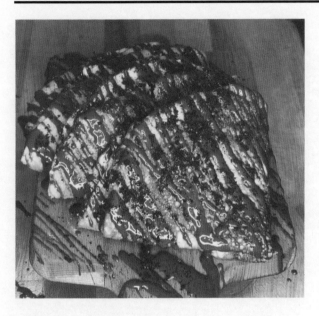

INGREDIENTS

70g banana

100g egg whites

1 scoop protein powder

Tsp. of baking powder

OPTIONAL toppings
(low cal chocolate spread
and oreo crumbs)

METHOD

· Add all your ingredients to a blender and blend into a thick batter.

· Add the batter evenly to the whole surface area of the pan.

· Leave it on medium heat in the pan for 5 mins on each side of the crepe.

· Add whatever toppings you like to your crepes.

Scan me !!

THE ZACK CHUG Cookbook

HIGH PROTEIN HEALTHY
BREAKFAST

Calories 450	**Carbs** 41g	**Protein** 38g	**Fat** 14g

INGREDIENTS:

50g bell pepper

20g spinach

75g egg whites

1 whole egg

50ml semi skimmed milk

20g mozzarella cheese

50g turkey slices (meat of choice)

Tortilla wrap

METHOD

- Add your pepper and spinach to a bowl followed by your egg whites and whole egg.

- Add in your milk and give this mixture a good whisk.

- Place a tortilla wrap in a rectangular baking dish so it forms a little tortilla basket.

- Pour your egg mixture into the wrap and top it off with cheese and your meat of choice.

- Bake in the oven or air fry at 220 °C for 15-20 mins.

THE ZACK CHUG Cookbook

Scan me !!

OVERNIGHT OATS

Calories	380	Carbs	44g	Protein	33g	Fat	8g

INGREDIENTS

60g frozen mixed berries

30g blended oats (oat flour)

100g fat free Greek yoghurt

Scoop of protein powder

75 ml unsweetened almond milk

10g chia seeds

Tsp. cinnamon

THE **ZACK CHUG** Cookbook

METHOD

- Firstly, microwave your mixed berries for 1 minute to form a compote.

- Then add it to oats, yoghurt, protein powder, milk, chia seeds and cinnamon.

- Mix well together and place in a fridge overnight.

Scan me !!

BATTER OATS

Calories 360	**Carbs** 32g	**Protein** 43g	**Fat** 6g

INGREDIENTS

30g oats

10g cocoa powder

Scoop of chocolate protein powder

150ml unsweetened almond milk

150g low fat Greek yoghurt

THE ZACK CHUG Cookbook

METHOD

· Blend your oats and cocoa powder into a fine like flour.

· Add milk and yoghurt to your blended cocoa oats.

· Mix well together and freeze for 1 hour or fridge overnight.

 Scan me !!

HIGH PROTEIN
FRENCH TOAST

Calories	400	**Carbs**	77g	**Protein**	33g	**Fat**	4g

INGREDIENTS

150g egg whites

125 unsweetened almond milk

Vanilla extract

Cinnamon

OPTIONAL berry compote (microwave frozen berries for 1 min)

METHOD

- Mix egg whites, milk, vanilla extract & cinnamon well together.

- Soak your pieces of bread in the mixture.

- Pan fry for 3 mins on medium heat for each side of the soaked bread.

- Optional to microwave frozen berries for 1 minute to produce berry compote to top it with.

THE **ZACK CHUG** Cookbook

Scan me !!

BREAKFAST BAGEL

| **Calories** 400 | **Carbs** 26g | **Protein** 33g | **Fat** 19g |

INGREDIENTS

Thin seeded bagel

40g avocado

2 cooked turkey rashers

1 medium fried egg

20g mozzarella cheese

THE ZACK CHUG Cookbook

METHOD

- Firstly, cook your turkey rashers and then fry your egg.

- Add these to a bagel, and then top it off with avocado and cheese.

- Grill the bagel for 5 mins at 220 °C.

Scan me !!

HIGH PROTEIN
CHOC FRAPPUCINO

Calories	170	Carbs	4g	Protein	25g	Fat	5g

(WITHOUT OPTIONAL TOPPINGS)

INGREDIENTS

Ice

Black coffee

1 scoop of chocolate protein powder

10g of cocoa powder

METHOD

- Add all the ingredients into a blender.

- Blend well together and finish with optional choc. sauce & whipped cream.

THE ZACK CHUG Cookbook

Scan me !!

LOW CALORIE FLUFFY ENGLISH
MUFFINS

Calories 93	**Carbs** 16g	**Protein** 5g	**Fat** 1g

THIS MAKES 6 PORTIONS. CARBS MENTIONED ARE PER MUFFIN.

INGREDIENTS

140g self raising flour

140g low fat Greek yoghurt

Tbsp. of sweetener or OPTIONAL sugar

METHOD

• Add self raising flour, low fat Greek yoghurt and tbsp of sweetener or optional sugar.

• Mix and knead on a floured surface into a ball & cut into 6 equal pieces and flatten out.

• Add to a pan on medium heat and heat for 3-4 mins on each side.

Scan me !!

THE ZACK CHUG Cookbook

DESSERTS

HIGH PROTEIN
ENERGY BITES

Calories 410	**Carbs** 46g	**Protein** 28g	**Fat** 13g

INGREDIENTS:

40g oats

1 scoop of protein powder

50g banana

15g peanut butter

Tsp. cinnamon

Desiccated coconut sprinkles (OPTIONAL)

METHOD

- Melt 15g of peanut butter firstly.

- Add all your ingredients into a mixing bowl.

- Mix well into balls.

- Freeze for 1-2 hours or leave in the fridge overnight.

Scan me !! ——————————

THE ZACK CHUG Cookbook

PROTEIN BARS

Calories	315	**Carbs**	26g	**Protein**	27g	**Fat**	11g

INGREDIENTS

30g oats

1 scoop chocolate protein powder

5g chia seeds

10g peanut butter

150ml unsweetened almond milk

THE
ZACK CHUG
Cookbook

METHOD

- Melt the peanut butter.

- Add the peanut butter and the remaining ingredients all together.

- Add to a tray, flatten, and fridge for 2-3 hours.

- Then cut and divide into equal bars.

Scan me !!

POPCORN

Calories	350	Carbs	20g	Protein	28g	Fat	16g

INGREDIENTS

30g popcorn

1 scoop of chocolate protein powder

10g of low-calorie maple syrup

10g of melted peanut butter

THE **ZACK CHUG** Cookbook

METHOD

· Melt the peanut butter.

· Add the syrup and protein powder to the melted peanut butter.

· Mix till you reach a sand like consistency, add water to this mixture until it's thick and gloopy.

· Then fold in the popcorn.

· Place in a fridge for 1-2 hours.

Scan me !!

SNICKERS BAR

Calories	270	Carbs	13g	Protein	17g	Fat	15g

INGREDIENTS

Half a medium banana (around 30-40g)

5g melted peanut butter

10g peanuts

½ scoop vanilla protein powder

10g cacao powder

Melted 5g of coconut oil

METHOD

· Slice a medium banana down the middle.

· Add 5g of melted peanut butter on top of the banana.

· Separately, melt the coconut oil, add the cacao & protein powder to it and mix well.

· Add water if it's still very thick. This will form a chocolate top sauce.

· Add the sauce on top of the banana and top it off with peanuts.

· Place in the fridge for 2-3 hours.

THE ZACK CHUG Cookbook

Scan me !!

FUDGE BROWNIE

| **Calories** 450 | **Carbs** 24g | **Protein** 48g | **Fat** 14g |

INGREDIENTS

1 scoop choc. protein powder

30g cup of cacao powder

Tsp. of bicarbonate soda

250g fat free Greek yoghurt

100ml of unsweetened almond milk

10g of dark choc chips

METHOD

- Add the dry ingredients (cacao & protein powder & bicarb soda into a bowl first and mix well together).

- Add the wet ingredients (yoghurt & almond milk) to the bowl of dry ingredients and mix well.

- Fold in the choc chips.

- Add the mixture to a baking tray and bake in the oven for 15-20 mins at 220 °C.

THE **ZACK CHUG** Cookbook

Scan me !!

HIGH PROTEIN
OREO BARS

Calories	330	**Carbs**	30g	**Protein**	35g	**Fat**	7g

INGREDIENTS

200g fat free Greek yoghurt

1 scoop of protein powder

2 crushed oreos

THE ZACK CHUG Cookbook

METHOD

• Add the yoghurt and protein powder to a bowl and mix.

• Add in your crushed oreos to the mix and transfer to a rectangular dish.

• Freeze for 1-2 hours.

Scan me !!

HIGH PROTEIN
CHOCOLATE CAKE

Calories 330	**Carbs** 20g	**Protein** 44g	**Fat** 7g

INGREDIENTS

10g cocoa powder

Scoop of chocolate protein powder

250g fat free Greek yoghurt

50ml unsweetened almond milk

Tsp. baking powder

OPTIONAL 5g dark choc chips

METHOD

• Add the dry powder ingredients into a bowl and mix well.

• Follow this by adding the wet ingredients to the dry ingredients.

• Mix until a thick consistency is formed.

• Top it off with dark choc chips.

• Bake in the oven at 220°C for 20 mins.

Scan me !!

THE ZACK CHUG Cookbook

HIGH PROTEIN BROWNIE
MOUSSE

Calories	250	Carbs	15g	Protein	34g	Fat	6g

METHOD

· Melt 8g of dark chocolate first.

· Add your protein powder, yoghurt, and milk to a bowl.

· Mix well and fold the melted chocolate into it.

· Freeze for 1 hour.

INGREDIENTS

8g dark chocolate

1 scoop of chocolate protein powder

150g fat free Greek yoghurt

40ml unsweetened almond milk

THE ZACK CHUG Cookbook

Scan me !!

HIGH PROTEIN GOOEY
BROWNIES

Calories 390   **Carbs** 18g   **Protein** 31g   **Fat** 15g

THE ZACK CHUG Cookbook

INGREDIENTS

20g cocoa powder

10g plain flour

1/4 Tsp. baking powder

1 scoop chocolate protein powder

1 egg

75 ml of unsweetened almond milk

OPTIONAL 10g of dark choc chips

METHOD

- Add all the ingredients into a bowl and mix until thick.

- Place into a baking tray and into an oven for 7 mins at 220°C.

Scan me !!

CHEESECAKE

| **Calories** 540 | **Carbs** 40g | **Protein** 40g | **Fat** 23g |

INGREDIENTS

1 whole egg

40g low fat cream cheese

100g of fat free Greek yoghurt

Tbsp. vanilla extract

Scoop vanilla protein powder

6 crushed lotus biscuits (or biscuits of choice)

Low cal. oil spray

THE **ZACK CHUG** Cookbook

METHOD

· Mix all your ingredients, apart from the biscuits, into a thick creamy mixture firstly.

· Crush 6 biscuits and flatten to the bottom of a baking tray using low cal. oil spray.

· Pour cheesecake mixture on top and spread evenly.

· OPTIONAL to add extra crushed biscuits on top.

· Add to oven for 8-10 mins at 220°C, heat for less if you want it creamier.

Scan me !!

HIGH PROTEIN CHOC CHIP
COOKIES

(FOR WHOLE BATCH)

Calories 410 **Carbs** 22g **Protein** 20g **Fat** 27g

INGREDIENTS

1 whole egg

20g blended oats (oat flour)

36g peanut butter

Tbsp. vanilla extract

¼ Tsp. baking powder

10g dark choc chips

METHOD

· Melt your peanut butter firstly.

· Add all your ingredients to a bowl and fold in the peanut butter.

· Mix well and add equal sizes to a baking tray.

· Oven for 5-10 mins at 180°C depending on how gooey you like it.

THE ZACK CHUG Cookbook

Scan me !!

HIGH PROTEIN OREO
MCFLURRY

Calories	250	**Carbs**	18g	**Protein**	25g	**Fat**	8g

INGREDIENTS

Lots of ice

200ml of unsweetened almond milk

1 scoop of vanilla protein powder

2 oreos

2g of xantham gum (OPTIONAL)

METHOD

- Add all the ingredients into a blender and blend until you get a nice thick consistency.

- Xantham gum is completely optional, I only use it to make the ice cream thicker.

THE **ZACK CHUG** Cookbook

Scan me !!

ICE-CREAM

Calories 220	**Carbs** 7g	**Protein** 27g	**Fat** 9g

INGREDIENTS

Lots of ice

200ml of unsweetened almond milk

1 scoop of vanilla protein powder

10g chocolate chips

5g of peanut butter

2g of xantham gum

METHOD

· Add all your ingredients to a blender and blend until thick and creamy.

· Xantham gum is completely optional, I only use it to make the ice cream thicker, but adding enough ice can also do this.

THE ZACK CHUG Cookbook

Scan me !!

MILKSHAKE

Calories	200	**Carbs**	3g	**Protein**	30g	**Fat**	7g

INGREDIENTS

15g cocoa powder

1 scoop of chocolate protein powder

200ml unsweetened almond milk

Ice

OPTIONAL low calorie chocolate sauce

METHOD

- Blend all your ingredients together.

- Blend until thick and creamy, add more ice if you want it thicker.

- Top it off with optional low cal choc sauce.

THE **ZACK CHUG** Cookbook

Scan me !!

HIGH PROTEIN
M&Ms McFLURRY

Calories 220   **Carbs** 13g   **Protein** 27g   **Fat** 6g

INGREDIENTS

200ml unsweetened almond milk

Lots of ice

15g of M&Ms

1 scoop of protein powder

OPTIONAL 2g of xantham gum

OPTIONAL low cal choc sauce

METHOD

· Add all your ingredients to a blender.

· Blend it all up and add more ice until thick enough.

· Xantham gum is optional, it just makes it creamier.

· Optional to top it off with low calorie chocolate sauce.

THE ZACK CHUG Cookbook

Scan me !!

HIGH PROTEIN FUDGE
HOT CHOC

Calories	260	**Carbs**	10g	**Protein**	29g	**Fat**	11g

INGREDIENTS

200 ml unsweetened almond milk

15g cocoa powder

10g of dark chocolate chips

Scoop of chocolate protein powder

OPTIONAL low fat whipped cream

OPTIONAL low cal chocolate sauce

METHOD

- Add all of your ingredients into a blender and blend.

- Optional to whisk the ingredients together too.

- Simmer the mix on low to medium heat for 5 mins.

- Optional to top it off with low fat whipped cream and low cal choc sauce.

THE ZACK CHUG Cookbook

Scan me !!

HIGH PROTEIN RICE
KRISPIES TREAT

Calories	300	Carbs	45g	Protein	30g	Fat	5g

INGREDIENTS

20g marshmallows

30g of rice krispies

1 protein powder
scoop

OPTIONAL unsweetened
almond milk

METHOD

· Add marshmallows to a pan on low heat for 5 mins.

· Then fold in your rice krispies and protein powder and mix it all together.

· If it is still thick, add in a splash of unsweetened almond milk.

· Flatten onto a tray and freeze for 1 hour.

Scan me !!

THE ZACK CHUG Cookbook

HIGH PROTEIN BROWNIE
SUNDAE

Calories	370	**Carbs**	21g	**Protein**	41g	**Fat**	12g

INGREDIENTS

20g cocoa powder

1 Scoop of chocolate protein powder

Pinch of bicarbonate soda

10g of nutella

100g fat free Greek yoghurt

100ml unsweetened almond milk

10g of dark choc chips

OPTIONAL scoop of low cal Ice cream

METHOD

· Mix all of your ingredients in a mixing bowl and mix until it is thick.

· Place in a baking dish and its optional to top it with extra dark choc chips.

· Oven for 15-20 mins at 220 °C.

· Optional again to top it off with a scoop of low cal ice cream, macros are without the ice cream included.

Scan me !!

THE ZACK CHUG Cookbook

CORNFLAKE CRUNCH

| **Calories** 500 | **Carbs** 43g | **Protein** 32g | **Fat** 20g |

INGREDIENTS

50g of dark chocolate

125ml of unsweetened almond milk

1 scoop of protein powder

30g of cornflakes

METHOD

- Heat your dark chocolate, almond milk and protein powder on a stove on medium heat for 5 mins.

- Stir it well and then fold in your cornflakes.

- Flatten the cornflake crunch and freeze for 1-2 hours.

THE **ZACK CHUG** Cookbook

Scan me !!

CHOCOLATE CONCRETE

Calories	410	**Carbs**	31g	**Protein**	45g	**Fat**	10g

INGREDIENTS

25g of cocoa powder

Scoop of chocolate protein powder

30g of oats

Tsp. of baking powder

150g of low fat Greek yoghurt

METHOD

· Blend cocoa powder, protein powder and oats together into a flour.

· Add in the low fat Greek yoghurt to the flour and mix it well.

· Flatten onto a baking dish and oven for 15 mins at 220°C.

· Optional to add stevia sweetener granules on top of the concrete.

THE ZACK CHUG Cookbook

Scan me !!

HIGH PROTEIN
POPCORN BAR

Calories 500	Carbs 40g	Protein 30g	Fat 22g

INGREDIENTS

50g of dark chocolate

150ml unsweetened almond milk

1 scoop of chocolate protein powder

20g of sweet popcorn

METHOD

- Add your dark chocolate, unsweetened almond milk and protein powder to a pan.

- Let it simmer on medium to high heat for 5 mins.

- Then let it cool for 1 minute and fold in your popcorn.

- Mix it all together, flatten it on a tray and freeze for 2 hours.

THE ZACK CHUG Cookbook

Scan me !!

FUDGE BROWNIE

| **Calories** 260 | **Carbs** 18g | **Protein** 30g | **Fat** 8g |

INGREDIENTS

Lots of ice

125ml of unsweetened almond milk

Scoop chocolate protein powder

15g of cocoa powder

1 low calorie fibre brownie

2g of xantham gum (OPTIONAL)

METHOD

- Blend all your ingredients together until thick and creamy.

- Optional to add xantham gum to make it more thick.

THE ZACK CHUG Cookbook

Scan me !!

BROWNIES

(FOR WHOLE MIX)

Calories 460	**Carbs** 33g	**Protein** 49g	**Fat** 15g

INGREDIENTS

20g cocoa powder

1 chocolate protein powder scoop

75ml unsweetened almond milk

200g low fat Greek yoghurt

10g of dark choc chips

1/2 Tsp. of baking powder

METHOD

- Mix your cocoa powder, protein powder, almond milk, Greek yoghurt, choc chips & baking powder into a thick consistency.

- Pour it into a baking dish and then add 2 low cal cookies to it.

- Oven or air fry for 15 mins at 220°C.

THE **ZACK CHUG** Cookbook

Scan me !!

McFLURRY

Calories	290	Carbs	24g	Protein	38g	Fat	6g

INGREDIENTS

Lots of Ice

60g strawberries

50g banana

Handful spinach

Cinnamon

100g low fat Greek yoghurt

100ml semi skimmed milk
(or milk of choice)

1 scoop of chocolate
protein powder

THE **ZACK CHUG** Cookbook

METHOD

· Blend all the ingredients together and add more ice if you want it thicker.

Scan me !!

MILKSHAKE

Calories 300   **Carbs** 14g   **Protein** 27g   **Fat** 14g

INGREDIENTS

Lots of ice

200ml of unsweetened almond milk

15g of smooth peanut butter

1 scoop of chocolate protein powder

10g of Reese's mini peanut butter cups

OPTIONAL low fat whipped cream

OPTIONAL low cal choc sauce

THE ZACK CHUG Cookbook

METHOD

· Blend all your ingredients together to form a thick milkshake.

· Optional to add extra ice to make it more thick.

· Top it off with optional whipped cream & low cal choc sauce.

Scan me !!

HIGH PROTEIN
MANGO LASSI

Calories	290	Carbs	31g	Protein	33g	Fat	3g

INGREDIENTS

60g mango

150g low fat Greek yoghurt

50g mango pulp

1 scoop of protein powder

200ml of unsweetened almond milk

METHOD

- Blend all of your ingredients together until you form a thick and creamy milkshake consistency.

- Add more almond milk if it is too thick and enjoy!

Scan me !!

THE **ZACK CHUG** Cookbook

KRISPY KREME

Calories 300	**Carbs** 32g	**Protein** 25g	**Fat** 9g

INGREDIENTS

FOR THE KRISPY KREME GLAZE:

20g stevia sweetener

Tbsp. low cal syrup

50g low fat Greek yoghurt

FOR DOUGHNUT BATTER:

35g oats

1 whole egg

100g low fat Greek yoghurt

Vanilla extract

Tsp. baking powder

METHOD

- Firstly, mix your stevia sweetener, low cal syrup and Greek yoghurt to form the krispy kreme glaze.

- Then blend your oats, egg, Greek yoghurt, vanilla extract and baking powder to form a thick doughnut batter consistency.

- Add the batter to your doughnut hole tray and oven or air fry for 10 mins at 220°C.

THE **ZACK CHUG** Cookbook

Scan me !!

BROWNIE CAKE

Calories	450	Carbs	42g	Protein	37g	Fat	16g

INGREDIENTS

1 whole egg

15g melted dark chocolate

25g oat flour

1 scoop of protein powder

100g fat free Greek yoghurt

Tsp. baking powder

Low cal fibre brownie bar

METHOD

- Firstly, melt your dark chocolate.

- Add an egg, oat flour, protein powder, Greek yoghurt & baking powder to the dark chocolate and mix well until thick.

- Add a low cal brownie to the mixture.

- Place in the oven or air fry 15 mins at 220°C.

THE ZACK CHUG Cookbook

Scan me !!

HIGH PROTEIN CHOCOLATE OREO

MCFLURRY

Calories 260 | **Carbs** 19g | **Protein** 25g | **Fat** 8g

INGREDIENTS

Lots of ice (feel free to add more ice if you want it thicker)

200ml of unsweetened almond milk

1 scoop of vanilla protein powder

2 oreos

10g cocoa powder

2g of xanthan gum (OPTIONAL, I only use it to make the ice cream thicker, but adding enough ice can do this anyways)

THE ZACK CHUG Cookbook

METHOD

- Blend until you get a nice thick and creamy consistency.

 Scan me !!

HIGH PROTEIN DOUBLE CHOC
BANANA BREAD

Calories	99	**Carbs**	12g	**Protein**	9g	**Fat**	2g

Carbs mentioned are per slice.

These measurements make 6 slices. These can be stored in the fridge if you want to keep them for the week

INGREDIENTS

100g mashed banana

10g cocoa powder

60g self raising flour

50g choc protein powder (can use vanilla)

Tsp. baking powder

130ml unsweetened almond milk

10g dark choc chips

OPTIONAL low cal chocolate sauce

METHOD

- Take mashed banana, cocoa powder, self raising flour, choc protein powder (can use vanilla) tsp. baking powder and unsweetened almond milk and mix into a thick batter.

Continued...

Scan me !!

- Pour into a greased baking dish and add 10g dark choc chips.

- Oven or air fry for 20-25 mins @ 200°C until soft and fluffy.

- Add optional low cal chocolate sauce.

- Cut into even slices (I was able to make 6).

Scan me !!

THE
ZACK CHUG
Cookbook

SMOOTHIES

SMOOTHIE

| **Calories** 310 | **Carbs** 26g | **Protein** 31g | **Fat** 8g |

INGREDIENTS:

Ice

100ml almond milk

1 scoop protein powder

80g spinach

50g banana

5g chia seeds

40g frozen blueberries

100g fat free Greek yoghurt

5g pumpkin seeds

METHOD

- Blend all ingredients together into a nice thick smoothie.

THE ZACK CHUG Cookbook

Scan me !!

HEALTHY GREENS PROTEIN
SMOOTHIE

Calories 360	**Carbs** 36g	**Protein** 34g	**Fat** 8g

INGREDIENTS

20g kale

20g spinach

1 scoop of vanilla protein powder

150g 0% fat Greek yoghurt

10g sunflower seeds

45g banana

30g blueberries

50g mango

THE ZACK CHUG Cookbook

METHOD

· Add all the ingredients into a blender and blend well.

· Optional to add ice if you want it thicker.

Scan me !!

165 CALORIE TESOTERONE BOOSTER
SMOOTHIE

Calories 165	Carbs 43g	Protein 1g	Fat 0g

INGREDIENTS:

30g red grapes

30g pineapple

5g honey

3g ginger

150ml pomegranate juice

METHOD

· Blend all the ingredients together and enjoy.

THE ZACK CHUG Cookbook

Scan me !!

180 CALORIE TESTOSTERONE BOOSTER
SMOOTHIE

Calories 180   **Carbs** 17g   **Protein** 4g   **Fat** 11g

INGREDIENTS

20g blackberries

30g bananas

20g spinach

30g avocados

10g pumpkin seeds

150ml coconut water

METHOD

- Blend all ingredients together until smooth.

- Optional to add ice to make it thicker.

THE **ZACK CHUG** Cookbook

Scan me !!

SMOOTHIE

Calories	290	Carbs	33g	Protein	31g	Fat	4g

INGREDIENTS

Lots of ice

200 ml of unsweetened almond milk

80g frozen blueberries

50g of banana

200g of low fat Greek yoghurt

15g of protein powder

METHOD

· Blend all your ingredients until thick and creamy.

· If your smoothie isn't thick enough, add more ice.

Scan me !!

THE ZACK CHUG Cookbook

SMOOTHIE

Calories	90	Carbs	16g	Protein	1g	Fat	2g

INGREDIENTS

30g pineapple

30g pomegranate

30g kale

30g bananas

200 ml fortified coconut milk

METHOD

- Blend all the ingredients together and add ice if you want it thicker.

THE ZACK CHUG Cookbook

Scan me !!

SMOOTHIE

| **Calories** 110 | **Carbs** 25g | **Protein** 2g | **Fat** 2g |

INGREDIENTS

100g raspberries

50g mangoes

50g apples

2g ginger

200ml fortified coconut milk

METHOD

- Blend all the ingredients together.

- Optional to add ice to make it thicker.

THE ZACK CHUG Cookbook

Scan me !!

SMOOTHIE

| Calories | 190 | Carbs | 30g | Protein | 2g | Fat | 2g |

INGREDIENTS

50g watermelon

60g banana

one medium kiwi

50g blueberries

170ml fortified coconut milk

THE ZACK CHUG Cookbook

METHOD

- Blend all the ingredients together into a thick smoothie.

- Optional to add ice to make it thicker.

Scan me !!

SMOOTHIE

Calories 130	Carbs 29g	Protein 1g	Fat 2g

INGREDIENTS

100g pineapple

60g apple

1g ginger

Squeeze of lime

180ml coconut milk

METHOD:

• Blend all the ingredients together.

• Optional to add ice if you want the smoothie thicker.

THE ZACK CHUG Cookbook

Scan me !!

WATERMELON TESTOSTERONE BOOSTER
SMOOTHIE

Calories 170   **Carbs** 40g   **Protein** 3g   **Fat** 0g

INGREDIENTS

30g strawberries

30g watermelon

1g ginger

30g blueberries

150ml cranberry juice

METHOD

- Blend all the ingredients together.

- Optional to add ice if you want it thicker.

THE ZACK CHUG Cookbook

Scan me !!

CHERRY TESTOSTERONE BOOSTER
SMOOTHIE

Calories 160	**Carbs** 38g	**Protein** 1g	**Fat** 0g

INGREDIENTS

30g raspberries

30g watermelon

1g ginger

30g apple

150ml cherry juice

METHOD

- Blend all the ingredients together to form a refreshing, healthy smoothie.

- Optional to add ice to make it thicker.

THE **ZACK CHUG** Cookbook

SMOOTHIE

Calories 570	**Carbs** 50g	**Protein** 60g	**Fat** 12g

INGREDIENTS

120g frozen blueberries

70g banana

45g protein powder (can use vanilla or chocolate)

5g honey

10g peanut butter

7g chia seeds

150g skyr yoghurt (if you don't have this use low fat Greek yoghurt)

250ml fortified @alpro coconut milk

METHOD

· Take all the ingredients and put them in blender. Blend into a creamy and thick smoothie high in antioxidants, vitamins and fibre.

THE ZACK CHUG Cookbook

MEAL PREPS

The ingredients used in these recipes are to make one big meal prep to then portion equally into 5 servings !

CHICKEN ALFREDO

| **Calories** 360 | **Carbs** 40g | **Protein** 38g | **Fat** 5g |

(Carbs per meal)

INGREDIENTS

5 chicken breasts (altogether total raw weight was 600g)

Paprika, garlic and salt seasonings

250g of uncooked pasta

Garlic paste

300ml of skimmed milk (or milk of choice)

50g mozzarella cheese

Parsley

Black pepper

THE ZACK CHUG Cookbook

 Scan me !!

METHOD

- Get your chicken breasts and season with paprika, garlic and salt and rub it all in well.

- Oven for 25-30 mins @ 180°C until it's nice and juicy.

- Whilst the chicken is in the oven, boil 250g of uncooked pasta for 15 mins.

- Whilst it's boiling add garlic paste to a pan on medium to high heat!!

- Then add skimmed milk, mozzarella cheese, parsley and black pepper.

- Let it simmer for 5 mins and then add in your drained pasta and stir well so the pasta can absorb all the alfredo sauce until it's nice and creamy.

- Add to your meal prep containers.

Scan me !!

THE ZACK CHUG Cookbook

LOADED FRIES

Calories 360	**Carbs** 20g	**Protein** 44g	**Fat** 10g

(Carbs per meal)

INGREDIENTS

500g raw uncooked white potato

Garlic oregano, and chilli powder

Seasoning garlic

Add 600g of lean beef mince to a pan (or your MEAT OF CHOICE)

Chopped tomatoes

Spring onions

100g of low fat mozzarella cheese

OPTIONAL to finish with sriracha

THE
ZACK CHUG
Cookbook

Scan me !!

METHOD

· Season your sliced potatoes with garlic, oregano, and chilli powder.

· Then oven or air fry for 20 - 25 mins at 220°C.

· Add your lean beef mince to a pan and let it brown on the pan for 10 mins on medium heat.

· Then add in your chopped tomatoes and spring onions.

· And then mozzarella cheese.

· Mix and simmer on low - medium heat for 10 mins.

· Add equal portions of fries and beef mince to your meal prep containers.

THE
ZACK CHUG
Cookbook

KFC RICE

Calories 350	**Carbs** 48g	**Protein** 32g	**Fat** 6g

(Carbs per meal)

INGREDIENTS

100g crushed cornflakes

Paprika and oregano seasoning

50-100ml hot sauce

600g of raw chicken breast

200g of washed uncooked rice

Tomato sauce

Coriander

70g chopped red bell pepper

2 cups of water (300ml -400ml roughly)

OPTIONAL sriracha, black beans, sweet corn and lettuce

THE ZACK CHUG Cookbook

Scan me !!

METHOD

- Crush your cornflakes and season paprika and oregano seasoning to the cornflakes.

- Then add the hot sauce to a separate bowl.

- Then cut your raw chicken breast into strips and then coat it in sauce first and then cornflakes.

- Then oven or air fry for 20 - 25 mins at 220°C.

- Meanwhile add your washed uncooked rice to a pan followed by tomato sauce, coriander and chopped red bell pepper along with roughly 2 cups of water (300ml -400ml roughly).

- Let it simmer on medium to high heat for 20 mins until the rice is fluffy.

- Add equal portions of rice and kfc chicken strips to your meal prep containers.

- OPTIONAL to finish with SRIRACHA, black beans, sweet corn and lettuce.

THE ZACK CHUG Cookbook

HIGH PROTEIN MEAL PREP
PIZZAS

| **Calories** 260 | **Carbs** 18g | **Protein** 22g | **Fat** 10g |

INGREDIENTS

100g oats

4 eggs

375g low fat Greek yoghurt

A lot of garlic powder

Tsp. baking powder

Tomato sauce

Oregano

50g total mozzarella cheese for both 2 bases

60g turkey pepperoni for both 2 pizza bases (can use your meat of choice, using chicken will up the protein)

THE ZACK CHUG Cookbook

 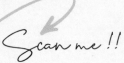

Scan me !!

METHOD

- Blend the oats into a fine like flour and add to a mixing bowl with your eggs.

- Followed by low fat Greek yoghurt, garlic powder and baking powder mix it well together and then oven or air fry for 20 - 25 mins at 220°C (works much better with an oven).

- Add equal portions of the mixture to 2 oven dishes.

- Once your pizza base is cooked, add tomato sauce and oregano to it.

- Then add your mozzarella cheese and turkey pepperoni to both 2 bases.

- Oven again for 5 mins at 180°C to melt your cheese.

- Then cut into slices and add equal portions to your meal prep containers.

TIKKA MASALA

Calories	330	**Carbs**	40g	**Protein**	32g	**Fat**	4g

INGREDIENTS

500g of raw chicken breast

Paprika

Turmeric

Salt

40g chopped onions

Tin of chopped tomatoes

300g low fat Greek yoghurt

Garlic paste

Tsp. of garam masala

Turmeric

Coriander/cilantro

625g of cooked pilau rice all together, I use packet pilau rice for ease

THE ZACK CHUG Cookbook

Scan me !!

METHOD

- Cut your raw chicken breast into pieces and season with paprika, turmeric and salt.

- Pan fry on medium to high heat or oven or air fry for 15 mins, use low cal oil spray to fry with.

- Add chopped onions to a pan, followed by tin of chopped tomatoes and then low fat Greek yoghurt, garlic paste, teaspoon of garam masala and turmeric.

- Leave it on low heat for 5 mins and then it's OPTIONAL to blend to form a thick and creamy paste.

- Then add your cooked chicken and coriander/cilantro.

- Mix it all together and serve with 125g of cooked packet pilau rice for each meal prep container.

THE
ZACK CHUG
Cookbook

DONNER KEBAB

Calories 350	**Carbs** 25g	**Protein** 45g	**Fat** 7g

FRIDGE UP TO 3 days or FREEZE for 3 months !!

INGREDIENTS

600g of raw lean beef mince (or meat of choice)

Garlic, oregano, cumin, coriander and parsley seasonings

100g low fat Greek yoghurt

Garlic paste or fresh garlic

Tsp. of mint sauce or use fresh mint leaves

1 pitta naan bread

Salad of choice (I used lettuce, tomato, onions and cucumber)

THE **ZACK CHUG** Cookbook

Scan me !!

METHOD

- Get your raw lean beef mince and season with garlic, oregano, cumin, coriander and parsley.

- Mix well and roll it out and then tightly seal with foil.

- Add to oven for 35-40 mins @ 200 °C.

- Once cooked, cut into into thin and juicy slices!!

FOR THE GARLIC SAUCE

- Mix low fat Greek yoghurt, garlic paste and mint sauce.

- Serve the kebab with a pitta naan bread and optional salad of choice.

- Drizzle your garlic mint sauce on top !

Scan me !!

THE ZACK CHUG Cookbook

CHICKEN CHOWMEIN

Calories 320	**Carbs** 40g	**Protein** 31g	**Fat** 4g

INGREDIENTS

600g of raw chicken breast

60ml light soy sauce

Garlic and black pepper seasoning

250g of uncooked noodles

Garlic paste

Red peppers

Spring onion

OPTIONAL sesame seeds

THE ZACK CHUG Cookbook

METHOD

- Dice your raw chicken breast into pieces and marinade with light soy sauce, garlic and black pepper and rub it all in well.

- Pan fry on medium to high heat for 15 mins until it's nice and sticky.

Continued..

Scan me !!

- Meanwhile boil 250g of uncooked noodles for 10mins.

- Whilst it's boiling add fresh ginger to a pan on medium to high heat and then garlic paste, red peppers & spring onion.

- Let it simmer and then add more light soy sauce, your cooked chicken and drained noodles.

- Stir it all together on low heat for 5 mins.

- Stir well so the noodles can absorb all chow mein sauce.

- Add to your meal prep containers with optional sesame seeds.

THE
ZACK CHUG
C o o k b o o k

HIGH PROTEIN MEAL PREP SWEET
CHILLI CHICKEN

| **Calories** | 300 | **Carbs** | 35g | **Protein** | 32g | **Fat** | 2g |

(Carbs per meal)

INGREDIENTS

600g of raw chicken breast

Garlic seasoning

Chilli flakes

Light soy sauce

Black pepper

200g of uncooked washed white rice

50g bell peppers

30g spring onions

Honey

Hot sauce

Ketchup

OPTIONAL sesame seeds

THE ZACK CHUG Cookbook

Scan me !!

METHOD

- Dice 600g of raw chicken breast into small pieces.

- Season with garlic, chilli flakes, light soy sauce and black pepper.

- Cook on the pan for 10-15 mins on medium to high heat.

- Boil your uncooked washed white rice (will work out to form 630g roughly of cooked white rice in the end).

- Add bell peppers, spring onions, soy sauce to a pan on medium heat and drizzle in your honey, hot sauce and ketchup.

- Let it simmer for 5-10 mins on low heat and add your cooked chicken.

- Add equal portions of rice (will roughly be 125g of cooked rice and chicken to each of your meal prep containers).

- Finish off with optional sesame seeds.

THE
ZACK CHUG
C o o k b o o k

FAJITA PASTA

Calories	370	**Carbs**	40g	**Protein**	37g	**Fat**	5g

INGREDIENTS

600g raw chicken breast

Chilli powder, basil, garlic and cumin

225g of uncooked penne pasta

40g chopped onions

50g bell peppers

Cayenne chilli
(can use normal chilli)

300 ml of skimmed milk
(or milk of choice)

50g mozzarella cheese

Parsley

THE **ZACK CHUG** Cookbook

Scan me !!

METHOD

- Dice 600g of raw chicken breast into small pieces.

- Then season with chilli powder, basil, garlic and cumin and then oven for 20-25 mins at 220 °C.

- Oven the chicken so whilst it's cooking you can then then boil 225g of uncooked penne pasta for 15 mins.

- Then add chopped onions & bell peppers to a pan on medium heat and season with cayenne chilli and cumin.

- Then add skimmed milk and mozzarella cheese.

- Simmer on high heat for 5 mins and then add in your cooked pasta and chicken.

- Give it a good stir and then garnish with parsley.

- Add equal portions to your meal prep containers.

Scan me !!

THE
ZACK CHUG
Cookbook

FRIED RICE

Calories 310   **Carbs** 33g   **Protein** 34g   **Fat** 4g

(Carbs per meal)

INGREDIENTS

200g of uncooked washed white rice (will work out to form 630g roughly of cooked white rice)

600g of raw chicken breast

Garlic

Light soy sauce

Black pepper

80g frozen veg

60g bell peppers

40g spring onions

2 whole eggs

OPTIONAL sesame seeds

THE ZACK CHUG Cookbook

Scan me !! ———

Chug

METHOD

- Firstly boil your uncooked washed white rice for 15 – 20 mins.

- Then dice your raw chicken breast into small cubes and season with garlic, light soy sauce and black pepper.

- Cook in the pan for 10-15 mins on medium to high heat .

- Then add frozen veg, bell peppers and spring onions to a pan and let it all sauté for 5 mins on high heat.

- Then add your whole eggs and quickly scrambled them together with the veg.

- Then add in your cooked rice, your cooked chicken and then a little bit of light soy sauce.

- Give it a good stir and add OPTIONAL Sesame seeds.

- Add equal portions (roughly) 125g of cooked rice and chicken to each of your meal prep containers.

- Freeze or refrigerate rice as soon It's cooked; fridge for up to 1/2 days and freeze the rest! Make sure it is STEAMING HOT when reheating.

LOADED NACHOS

Calories 400	**Carbs** 22g	**Protein** 42g	**Fat** 17g

(Carbs per meal)

INGREDIENTS

40g chopped onions

600g raw lean beef mince
(or meat of your choice)

Paprika, garlic, cumin,
ground coriander and chilli
flake seasoning

Chopped tomatoes

40g sweetcorn

50g of mozzarella cheese

150g nachos needed all
together

Sriracha sauce

25g chopped avocado

METHOD

- Add chopped onions to a pan and let it simmer for 5 mins on high heat.

- Then add 600g raw lean beef mince and season with paprika, garlic, cumin, ground coriander and chill flakes.

- Let it brown in the pan for 10 mins on medium heat then add chopped tomatoes followed by sweetcorn and mozzarella cheese.

Continued..

Scan me !!

THE ZACK CHUG Cookbook

- Let it brown on the pan for 10 mins on medium heat then add chopped tomatoes followed by sweetcorn and mozzarella cheese.

- Let it simmer for 5-10 mins on medium heat and add equal portions to your meal prep containers.

- Add 30g of nachos to each container and top it off with your cooked mince meat.

- Top with sriracha sauce and 5g chopped avocado per container.

THE ZACK CHUG Cookbook

CHICKEN SHAWARMA

Calories 300 **Carbs** 25g **Protein** 32g **Fat** 3g

Carbs mentioned are per meal. Store the meals in the fridge up to 3 days or keep it frozen up to 3 months

INGREDIENTS

600g white raw potatoes

100g low fat Greek yoghurt

Garlic powder

Oregano

Paprika

Cinnamon

Cumin

Garlic paste

Tomato paste

Onions

Red cabbage & pickles
(OPTIONAL)

THE ZACK CHUG Cookbook

Scan me !!

METHOD

- Get 600g uncooked white raw potatoes and season with garlic powder and oregano.

- Mix well and oven or Air fry for 20 mins -40 mins @ 220°C.

- Then season your 600g raw chicken breast with paprika, garlic powder, cinnamon & cumin.

- Then add tomato paste and chopped onions and stir together on medium to high heat for 10-15 mins.

- Top it off with optional salad (I went red cabbage and pickles) and low calorie garlic sauce.

LOW CALORIE GARLIC SAUCE

- Mix 100g low fat Greek yoghurt.

- Add garlic paste or fresh garlic.

BURRITO BOWL

Calories	360	Carbs	136g	Protein	35g	Fat	7g

Carbs mentioned are per meal. Store the meals in the fridge up to 3 days or keep it frozen upto 3 months

INGREDIENTS

650g raw chicken breast

225 uncooked white rice

30g avocado

300-400ml water

Garlic powder

Coriander

Chilli powder

Cinnamon

Cumin

Sweet corns

Tomato sauce

Sriracha sauce
(OPTIONAL)

THE **ZACK CHUG** Cookbook

Scan me !!

METHOD

- Get 650g raw chicken breast.

- Season with cumin, chilli powder & garlic powder.

- Mix well and oven or Air fry for 25 mins @ 180°C.

- Once cooked dice into little chicken cubes.

- Whilst the chicken is cooking add 225g uncooked washed white rice to a pan with tomato sauce, coriander and 300-400ml water roughly 2 cups.

- Add turmeric.

- Boil for 20 mins on high heat and then stir in sweetcorn.

- Serve with optional Salad (I used onions, tomato and coriander) & 30g smashed avocado & sriracha sauce.

THE
ZACK CHUG
Cookbook

RAMEN NOODLES

Calories	360	Carbs	40g	Protein	35g	Fat	5g

Carbs mentioned are per meal. Store the meals in the fridge up to 3 days or keep it frozen up to 3 months

INGREDIENTS

600g raw chicken breast

Tsp. garlic powder

Tsp. paprika

Tsp. ground ginger

Tsp. cinnamon

50ml light soy sauce

Tbsp. garlic & ginger paste spring onions

Red chilli (to taste preference)

Light soy sauce

One chicken or veg stock cube dissolved in 700ml-800ml

250g of uncooked ramen noodles or noodles of choice

OPTIONAL sesame seeds

METHOD

• Season your chicken breast with garlic powder, paprika, ground ginger, cinnamon and soy sauce to give it a nice Chinese five spices flavouring.

• Mix well and rub in well till a thick paste marinade forms on the chicken.

Continued..

Scan me !!

THE ZACK CHUG Cookbook

- Oven or air fry for 20 mins @ 200°C.

- Then add garlic & ginger paste to a pan on medium heat followed by spring onions, red chilli, light soy sauce, and one chicken or veg stock cube dissolved in 700ml-800ml of boiling water.

- Then your noodles to the pan and let it simmer for 10 mins on high heat.

- Stir well together and add to your noodles and chicken.

- Divide your noodle & chicken portions up equally per container.

THE
ZACK CHUG
Cookbook

HIGH PROTEIN MEAL PREP
BUTTER CHICKEN

Calories	320	**Carbs**	35g	**Protein**	35g	**Fat**	5g

Carbs mentioned are per meal. Store the meals in the fridge up to 2 days or keep it frozen in the freezer up to 3 months

INGREDIENTS

600g raw chicken breast

200g of uncooked washed rice

200g low fat Greek yoghurt

60g low fat cream cheese

Turmeric

Garam masala

Paprika

Tomato purée / sauce

Chopped onions

Coriander

THE **ZACK CHUG** Cookbook

Scan me !!

METHOD

- Cut your 600g of raw chicken breast into pieces.

- Season with paprika, turmeric and garam masala.

- Then add 200g low fat Greek yoghurt and mix well.

- Cook for 15-20 mins on high heat or oven or air fry for 20 mins at 200°C.

- Meanwhile your chicken is cooking, boil 200g of uncooked washed rice (will work out to roughly 630g of cooked rice).

- Then to a pan on medium heat add chopped onions, garlic paste, tomato purée /sauce and turmeric.

- Add 60g low fat cream cheese.
  (used this so blending is NOT NECESSARY)

- Then stir well until nice and creamy or OPTIONAL to blend it all together.

- Then add your cooked chicken and coriander.

- Serve it all up with roughly 125g of cooked rice in each container and optional to top with yoghurt and coriander.

- ENJOY.

THE **ZACK CHUG** Cookbook

HONEY GARLIC CHICKEN

Calories 320	**Carbs** 37g	**Protein** 33g	**Fat** 4g

(CARBS PER MEAL)

INGREDIENTS

600g of diced raw chicken breast

Tsp. of chilli powder, garlic powder, black pepper

50ml light soy sauce

200g of uncooked white rice

Tsp. of coconut oil or you can use low cal oil spray

Spring onions

Tbsp. garlic paste

75ml soy sauce (add water if more volume to sauce needed)

Hot sauce

Honey

OPTIONAL sesame seeds

THE ZACK CHUG Cookbook

Scan me !!

METHOD

- Season your diced chicken with a teaspoon of chilli powder, garlic powder, black pepper & light soy sauce and mix it well together.

- Cook on the pan for 10-15 mins on medium to high heat! You can instead oven or air fry the chicken for 20 mins @ 220 °C.

- Then boil the uncooked washed white rice whilst cooking your chicken.

- To a separate pan on medium heat, add coconut oil or low cal oil spray followed by spring onions, garlic paste, soy sauce, Hot sauce and a drizzle of honey.

- Then add your cooked chicken and let it all simmer for 5-10 mins on low heat and stir well together.

- Finish with optional sesame seeds.

THE
ZACK CHUG
Cookbook

Scan me !!

LOADED FRIES

| **Calories** 300 | **Carbs** 25g | **Protein** 35g | **Fat** 8g |

Carbs mentioned are per meal. Store the meals in the fridge up to 3 days or keep it frozen up to 3 months

INGREDIENTS

600g raw white potato

Tsp. oregano, garlic and chilli powder seasoning

650g of raw chicken breast

Paprika and garlic

Spring onions

60g hot sauce

30g light mayo

60g of low fat mozzarella cheese

OPTIONAL to finish with sriracha

THE ZACK CHUG Cookbook

Scan me !!

METHOD

- Slice 600g raw uncooked white potato into fries and season with oregano, garlic and chilli powder seasoning.

- Mix well and oven or air fry for 20 - 25 mins @ 220°C.

- Season your raw chicken breast with paprika and garlic and add to a pan on medium heat for 10 mins.

- Then add spring onions, hot sauce, light mayo and low fat mozzarella cheese.

- Mix and simmer on low - medium heat for 5 mins until rich and creamy.

- Add equal portions of fries and chicken to your meal prep containers and OPTIONAL to finish with SRIRACHA.

THE
ZACK CHUG
Cookbook

Scan me !!

HIGH PROTEIN MEAL PREP
CHICKEN KEBAB

Calories 360 **Carbs** 40g **Protein** 35g **Fat** 5g

Carbs mentioned are per meal. Store the meals in the fridge up to 2 days or keep it frozen up to 3 months

INGREDIENTS

200g low fat Greek yoghurt

Tsp. of olive oil

Garlic paste

Tsp. chilli powder

Tsp. of cumin

Lemon juice

600g of diced chicken breast

200g of uncooked washed rice

FOR YOUR WHITE GARLIC SAUCE:

100g low fat Greek yoghurt

Tsp. mint sauce or fresh mint

Tsp. garlic paste or minced garlic

Coriander

OPTIONAL mixed salad (tomato, parsley, and onions)

THE **ZACK CHUG** Cookbook

Scan me !!

METHOD

- Get 600g of raw chicken breast cubes and marinade it well with olive oil, low fat Greek yoghurt, garlic paste, chilli powder, cumin and lemon juice.

- Oven or Air fry for 20 -25 mins @ 200°C 1 or you can cook on a pan for 10-15 mins on high heat.

- Whilst your chicken is cooking, boil the uncooked washed rice.

- For your white garlic sauce mix your low fat Greek yoghurt, mint sauce, garlic paste and coriander.

- Serve it all up with roughly 125g of cooked rice in each container and optional to have mixed salad (I went with tomato, parsley and onions).

Scan me !!

THE
ZACK CHUG
C o o k b o o k

MAC & CHEESE

Calories 370 **Carbs** 38g **Protein** 37g **Fat** 6g

Carbs mentioned are per meal. Store the meals in the fridge up to 3 days or keep it frozen up to 3 months

INGREDIENTS

Chicken or meat of choice

Pasta macaroni

Garlic paste

300ml milk of choice

Paprika

30g mozzarella

20g cheddar cheese

Chilli powder

Black pepper

Garlic powder

30g low fat cream cheese

THE ZACK CHUG Cookbook

Scan me !!

METHOD

- Dice 600g raw chicken breast into pieces.

- Season with a tsp. of chilli powder, black pepper and a garlic powder.

- Mix well together and pan fry on medium heat for 10-15 minutes.

- At the same time boil 250g uncooked pasta macaroni for 10 mins.

- On low heat to a pan add a tablespoon of garlic paste , milk of choice, paprika & low fat cream cheese.

- Add mozzarella & cheddar cheese.

- Mix well together and then add your cooked pasta and a splash of hot sauce.

- Add your cooked chicken and then mix well.

- Garnish with parsley and optional black pepper.

- Add equal portions to your to your meal prep containers.

THE ZACK CHUG Cookbook

CHILLI GARLIC NOODLES

Calories 330   **Carbs** 30g   **Protein** 33g   **Fat** 8g

Carbs mentioned are per meal. Store the meals in the fridge up to 3 days or keep it frozen upto 3 months

INGREDIENTS

600g raw diced chicken breast

Minced garlic

Chilli flakes

80ml light soy auce

Tbsp. sesame oil

240g uncooked noodles

Siracha sauce

Tsp. sesame seeds

THE ZACK CHUG Cookbook

Scan me !!

METHOD

- Add minced garlic, chilli flakes, 80ml light soy sauce and diced chicken mix it all together.

- Pan fry for 10-15 mins on high heat (or oven / air fry @ 220°C for 1 mins).

- Add the leftover sauce in the pan from cooking the chicken to separate pan on medium heat.

- Add a tablespoon of sesame oil.

- Add soy sauce & teaspoon of sesame seeds.

- Let it simmer and add 750g cooked noodles (roughly 240grams uncooked noodles), followed by minced garlic & your cooked chicken.

- Stir together well and add optional spring onions.

- Add equal portions to our to your meal prep containers.

THE
ZACK CHUG
Cookbook

CHEESEBURGERS

| Calories | 370 | Carbs | 33g | Protein | 40g | Fat | 9g |

Keep it frozen in the freezer & thaw in fridge the night before you want to eat it and reheat the next day. The ingredients used in this is to make one big meal prep to then portion equally into 6 burgers

INGREDIENTS

600g raw lean beef mince (meat of choice)

Brioche bun

Garlic powder, paprika, black Pepper & Salt

Cheese slices

50g low fat greek yoghurt

Tbsp. ketchup

Tbsp. mustard

Oregano

Gherkins

THE
ZACK CHUG
C o o k b o o k

METHOD

- Add 600g raw lean beef mince (or meat mince of choice) to a bowl.

- Season with garlic powder, paprika, black pepper & salt.

Continued..

Scan me !!

- Mix it together, first form into equal balls and then smash into patties.

- Pan fry for 2-3 mins on high heat (or oven / air fry @ 220°C for 10-15 mins.

- Add a light cheese slice to each patty on the pan & leave to melt for 1 mins on high heat.

FOR THE HEALTHY BURGER SAUCE

- 50g low fat Greek yoghurt (makes it creamy & healthier than mayo).

- Add a tablespoon ketchup & tablespoon mustard.

- Add chopped gherkins & mix well.

- Add your patties and sauce to a toasted brioche bun.

- Tightly seal each burger in foil and store in the freezer.

THE ZACK CHUG Cookbook

FLUFFY PANCAKES

Calories	220	**Carbs**	12g	**Protein**	22g	**Fat**	9g

Carbs mentioned are per meal. Store the pancakes in the fridge up to 3 days or keep it frozen in the freezer & reheat using a toaster

INGREDIENTS

6 large eggs

90g vanilla protein powder

200g banana

Tsp. of baking powder

METHOD

- Blend it all together.

- Add equal portions of batter onto the pan and cook for 2-3 mins on medium heat.

- Should make roughly 15 pancakes.

- Portion the servings equally based on how many pancakes you make.

- Use baking paper to separate pancakes so it's easy to compartmentalise when storing in the freezer or fridge.

- Add optional low cal chocolate sauce when reheated or toppings of choice.

Scan me !!

THE ZACK CHUG Cookbook

PERI PERI BURGERS

| **Calories** 340 | **Carbs** 33g | **Protein** 31g | **Fat** 6g |

Keep it frozen in the freezer & thaw in fridge the night before you want to eat it and reheat the next day. The ingredients used in this is to make one big meal prep to then portion equally into 6 burgers

INGREDIENTS

600g raw chicken breast

Garlic powder paprika, chilli flakes and oregano

Light cheese slice

50g low fat Greek yoghurt

Tbsp. sriracha

Tbsp. mustard

Brioche bun

METHOD

- Get 600g Raw chicken breast and slice into thin fillets.

- Season with garlic powder, paprika, chilli flakes and oregano.

- Mix it together & oven / air fry @ 220°C for 15 mins.

- Add a light cheese slice to each chicken fillet & leave to melt for 1 min!!

FOR THE HEALTHY NANDOS PERINAISE SAUCE

- 50g low fat Greek yoghurt (makes it creamy & healthier than mayo tablespoon sriracha & tablespoon mustard)

THE ZACK CHUG Cookbook

Scan me !!

Continued..

- Add oregano & mix well.

- Add your chicken and cheese and sauce to a toasted brioche bun.

- Tightly seal each burger in foil and store in the freezer.

THE ZACK CHUG Cookbook

Scan me !!

BREAKFAST MCMUFFINS

| **Calories** 420 | **Carbs** 33g | **Protein** 42g | **Fat** 6g |

Keep it frozen in the freezer & thaw in fridge the night before you want to eat it and reheat the next day. The ingredients used in this is to make one big meal prep to then portion equally into 6 burgers

INGREDIENTS

500g raw lean beef mince

Black pepper, salt, garlic powder & paprika

Light cheese slices

6 eggs

METHOD

- Add 500g raw lean beef mince in a bowl.

- Season with black pepper, salt, garlic powder & paprika.

- Mix it together & form small balls and smash into patties.

- Cook in the pan on high heat for 2-3 mins each side of the patty.

- Add a light cheese slice to each patty & leave to melt for 1 min.

Continued..

THE ZACK CHUG Cookbook

Scan me !!

FOR YOUR EGGS

- Add 6 medium whole eggs to a baking dish.

- Pop the yolk & oven / air fry @ 220°C for 10 mins.

- Cut into squares or circles whichever you prefer.

- Add your patty and cheese and egg to a toasted muffin.

- Tightly seal each burger in foil and store in the freezer.

THE
ZACK CHUG
Cookbook

LOADED FRIES

Calories 360	**Carbs** 22g	**Protein** 49g	**Fat** 8g

Carbs mentioned are per meal. Store the meals in the fridge up to 3 days or keep it frozen up to 3 months

INGREDIENTS

500g raw uncooked white potato

Garlic, paprika & oregano seasoning

600g of lean turkey mince (or meat of choice)

Spring onions

Chopped tomatoes

50g of low-fat mozzarella cheese

5 eggs

METHOD

- Slice 500g raw uncooked white potato into fries.

- Garlic, paprika & oregano seasoning.

- Oven or air fry for 20 - 25 mins @ 220°C.

Continued..

Scan me !!

THE **ZACK CHUG** Cookbook

- Add 600g of lean turkey mince to a pan (or your MEAT OF CHOICE like beef or chicken mince).

- Let it brown on the pan for 10 mins on high heat and add in paprika, chopped tomatoes, spring onions.

- And then 50g of low fat mozzarella cheese.

- Simmer on low - medium heat for 10 mins.

- Then cook your 5 eggs on medium heat and serve equally on top of your fries and turkey mince.

- Add equal portions of fries and turkey mince to your meal prep containers and OPTIONAL to finish with SRIRACHA & PARSLEY.

Scan me !!

THE
ZACK CHUG
Cookbook

CHICKEN GYROS

Calories 310	**Carbs** 25g	**Protein** 35g	**Fat** 6g

Carbs mentioned are per meal. Store the meals in the fridge up to 3 days or keep it frozen up to 3 months

INGREDIENTS

600g raw chicken breast

Tbsp. olive oil

Garlic

Lemon juice

100g low fat Greek yoghurt

Chilli powder

Cumin

Oregano

50g low fat Greek yoghurt

Cucumbers and fresh mint

Pitta bread

FULL RECIPE NEXT PAGE

Scan me !!

THE ZACK CHUG Cookbook

METHOD

- Add chicken to a bowl and marinade with tbsp olive oil, garlic, lemon juice.

- Add 100g low fat Greek yoghurt.

- Add chilli powder, cumin, and oregano seasoning.

- Oven or air fry for 15 - 20 mins @ 200°C and then cut it equally into juicy slices.

FOR THE TZATZIKI SAUCE

- Add low fat Greek yoghurt, cucumbers, garlic and mint sauce or fresh mint.

- Mix together.

- Serve the chicken and sauce with one pitta bread for each meal prep along with optional salad (I used cucumber and tomato).

THE
ZACK CHUG
Cookbook

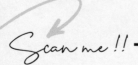

FAJITA WRAPS

Calories 340   **Carbs** 34g   **Protein** 35g   **Fat** 7g

Carbs mentioned are per meal. Store the meals in the fridge up to 3 days or keep it frozen up to 3 months

INGREDINTS

600g raw chicken breast

Wrap bread

Tsp. chilli powder, garlic, cumin, and lime juice

Onions

Bell peppers

30g mozzarella cheese

100g low fat Greek yoghurt

30g avocado

Coriander & garlic

THE **ZACK CHUG** Cookbook

METHOD

• Add 600g of raw chicken breast into a bowl.

• Season with tsp. chilli powder, garlic, cumin, and lime juice.

• Mix well together and cook on medium heat on a pan for 10 mins.

Continued..

Scan me !!

- Then add onions, bell peppers and 30g mozzarella cheese.

- Let it simmer for 5 mins on low heat.

FOR THE HEALTHY FAJITA SAUCE

- Add 100g low fat Greek yoghurt, coriander, 30g avocado and garlic into a blender.

- Blend together.

- Serve the chicken and sauce with one wrap bread for each meal prep and tightly seal with foil.

THE
ZACK CHUG
Cookbook

CAJUN PASTA

Calories 350　**Carbs** 40g　**Protein** 37g　**Fat** 4g

Carbs mentioned are per meal. Store the meals in the fridge up to 3 days or keep it frozen up to 3 months

INGREDIENTS

600g raw chicken breast

250g uncooked pasta

50g mozzarella cheese

Tbsp. paprika

Tbsp. garlic powder

Oregano

Chilli flakes

Chopped onions

Bell peppers

300ml of skimmed milk
(or milk of choice)

Parsley

FULL RECIPE NEXT PAGE

THE ZACK CHUG Cookbook

Scan me !!

METHOD

- Take 600g of raw chicken breast and season with tbsp. paprika, tbsp. garlic powder, oregano, and chill flakes.

- Rub it all in well.

- Oven for 15-20 mins @ 220°C until it's nice and juicy and cut into pieces.

- Boil 250g of uncooked pasta for 15 mins.

- Whilst it's boiling add garlic paste, chopped onions and bell peppers to a pan on medium to high heat.

- Then add 300ml of skimmed milk (or milk of choice).

- Add 50g mozzarella cheese and parsley.

- Let it simmer for 5 mins and then add in your drained pasta and stir well so the pasta can absorb all the cajun sauce until it's nice and creamy.

- Add to your meal prep containers.

THE
ZACK CHUG
Cookbook

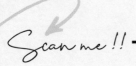
Scan me !!

BUTTER GARLIC CHICKEN

Calories 330   **Carbs** 35g   **Protein** 32g   **Fat** 9g

Carbs mentioned are per meal. Store the meals in the fridge up to 3 days or keep it frozen up to 3 months

INGREDIENTS

600g raw chicken breast

30g light butter

Tbsp. olive oil

Garlic powder

Tsp. paprika

Black pepper

Tbsp. garlic paste

Drizzle of honey

Coriander

Chilli flakes

200g uncooked white rice

FULL RECIPE NEXT PAGE

THE
ZACK CHUG
Cookbook

Scan me !! ——————

METHOD

- Slice 600g raw chicken breast into small pieces.

- Season with tbsp. olive oil, tbsp. garlic powder, teaspoon paprika, black pepper and mix it all together.

- At medium heat on a pan add 30g light butter and tbsp. garlic paste.

- Add your seasoned raw chicken from before, drizzle of honey, coriander & chilli flakes.

- Cook the chicken for 15 mins and let it simmer until it's all sticky and thick.

- Whilst preparing your chicken, BOIL 200g uncooked washed white rice (roughly will form 630g cooked rice).

- Add equal portions to your meal prep containers (roughly 125g cooked rice per container)

THE **ZACK CHUG** Cookbook

Scan me !!

PARMESAN CHICKEN

| **Calories** 390 | **Carbs** 40g | **Protein** 39g | **Fat** 9g |

Carbs mentioned are per meal. Store the meals in the fridge up to 3 days or keep it frozen up to 3 months

INGREDIENTS

600g raw chicken breast

Tbsp. garlic Powder

Tbsp. oregano

Tsp. onion powder

Tsp. paprika

Tbsp. olive oil

30g light butter

300ml skimmed milk or milk of choice

25g parmesan cheese

30g low fat cream cheese

Chopped onions

Tbsp. garlic paste

200g -250g uncooked pasta

Parsley

FULL RECIPE NEXT PAGE

Scan me !!

THE ZACK CHUG Cookbook

METHOD

- Season 600g raw chicken breast with garlic powder, oregano, onion powder and tsp. paprika and olive oil.

- Mix it all together.

- Cook for 15 mins on medium heat on a pan, set the chicken aside and then to the same pan add light butter, garlic paste and chopped onions.

- Add 300ml skimmed milk or milk of choice, low fat cream cheese, parmesan cheese, parsley and 600g of already cooked pasta.
(in the background whilst preparing your chicken, BOIL 200g -250g roughly of uncooked pasta)

- Add the cooked chicken and simmer until it's all nice and creamy.

- Add equal portions to your meal prep containers.

THE
ZACK CHUG
C o o k b o o k

Scan me !!

KATSU CURRY

Calories	310	Carbs	35g	Protein	31g	Fat	7g

Carbs mentioned are per meal. Store the meals in the fridge up to 3 days or keep it frozen up to 3 months

INGREDIENTS

600g raw chicken breast

300ml chicken stock

200g of uncooked washed white rice

30g chopped onions

Tbsp. light soy sauce

Tbsp. cumin

Tsp. chilli powder

Chopped garlic

10g roughly of honey

Tsp. turmeric and black pepper

FULL RECIPE NEXT PAGE

METHOD

- Get 600g raw chicken breast and season with tbsp. light soy sauce, tbsp. cumin, tsp. chilli powder and tsp. turmeric and black pepper.

- Oven or air fry at 220°C for 15 mins until golden brown.

- On medium heat on a pan, add chopped garlic, 30g chopped onions, tsp. ginger and cumin.

- Add 300ml chicken stock , soy sauce and drizzle of honey.

- Let it simmer for 5 mins and blend until nice and thick with a hand blender or Nutribullet.

- Whilst doing all of this, boil 200g of uncooked washed white rice (roughly forms 630g of cooked rice).

- Add equal portions to your meal prep containers (roughly 125g of cooked rice to each container).

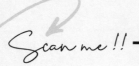

Scan me !!

THE
ZACK CHUG
Cookbook

SPICY GARLIC NOODLES

Calories 360	**Carbs** 31g	**Protein** 35g	**Fat** 9g

Carbs mentioned are per meal. Store the meals in the fridge up to 3 days or keep it frozen up to 3 months

INGREDIENTS

600g raw chicken breast

Low calorie oil spray

30g light butter

130ml light soy sauce

300ml skimmed milk or milk of choice

240g uncooked noodles

Tbsp. tomato paste

Tbsp. garlic paste

Sriracha sauce

Tsp. chilli flakes

30g low fat cream cheese

20g parmesan cheese

FULL RECIPE NEXT PAGE

THE **ZACK CHUG** Cookbook

Scan me !!

METHOD

- Add tbsp. garlic paste, sriracha sauce, 50ml light soy sauce teaspoon chilli flakes to a bowl.

- Then add 600g raw chicken breast and mix it well together.

- Pan fry using low cal oil spray for 10-15 mins on high heat or (oven or air fry at 220°C for 15 mins until golden brown.

- On medium heat on a pan add 30g light butter, chopped garlic and tbsp. of tomato paste.

- Add 80ml light soy sauce and skimmed milk of choice and low fat cream cheese and parmesan cheese.

- Add 750g cooked noodles (roughly 240g uncooked noodles).

- Add cooked chicken from before and optional coriander.

- Let it simmer for 5 mins and stir well until rich and creamy.

- Add equal portions to your meal prep containers.

THE
ZACK CHUG
Cookbook

Scan me !!

HIGH PROTEIN MEAL PREP GARLIC
TUSCAN CHICKEN

Calories 390	**Carbs** 40g	**Protein** 38g	**Fat** 9g

Carbs mentioned are per meal. Store the meals in the fridge up to 3 days or keep it frozen up to 3 months

INGREDIENTS

600g raw chicken breast

300ml skimmed milk or milk of choice

30g low fat cream cheese

20g parmesan cheese

200g - 250g uncooked pasta

30g light butter

Tbsp. olive oil

Tbsp. oregano

Tbsp. garlic powder

Tsp. paprika

Chopped baby tomatoes

Tbsp. tomato paste

Chopped spinach and garlic

FULL RECIPE NEXT PAGE

THE **ZACK CHUG** Cookbook

Scan me !!

METHOD

- Get 600g raw chicken breast and season with tbsp. olive oil, tbsp. oregano, tbsp. garlic powder and teaspoon of paprika.

- Mix it well together.

- Pan fry using low cal oil spray for 10-15 mins on high heat or (oven or air fry at 220°C for 15 mins until golden brown) and then set your chicken to one side.

- On medium heat on the same pan, add 30g light butter, chopped garlic, chopped baby tomatoes and tablespoon tomato paste.

- Add 300ml skimmed milk or milk of choice and 30g low fat cream cheese & 20g parmesan cheese.

- Then add chopped spinach.

- Add 600g of already cooked pasta (in the background whilst prepping your chicken, BOIL 200g - 250g roughly of uncooked pasta).

- Add your cooked chicken and let it simmer until rich and creamy.

- Add equal portions to your meal prep containers.

HIGH PROTEIN MEAL PREP
JUICY KOFTAS

Calories 350	**Carbs** 36g	**Protein** 35g	**Fat** 6g

Carbs mentioned are per meal. Store the meals in the fridge up to 3 days or keep it frozen up to 3 months

INGREDIENTS

600g raw lean beef mince or meat of choice

100g low fat Greek yoghurt

200g - 250g uncooked white rice

Tsp. cumin

Tbsp. tomato

Bell pepper

Parsley and onions

Tsp. olive

Coriander & garlic

Tbsp. garlic paste

Lemon juice

Tsp. mint sauce

FULL RECIPE NEXT PAGE

THE **ZACK CHUG** Cookbook

Scan me !!

METHOD

- Add raw lean beef mince to a bowl.

- Season with garlic, cumin, and tomato paste.

- Add finely chopped bell pepper, parsley and onions.

- Mix it well together and roll into a small baby kofta shape.

- Add a teaspoon of olive oil to a pan and fry the koftas as for 10-15 mins on medium to high heat until juicy and golden (oven or air fry at 220°C for 15 mins until golden brown).

FOR THE WHITE SAUCE

- Add low fat Greek yoghurt, coriander, tbsp. garlic paste, lemon juice and tsp. mint sauce

- Mix well until thick.

- Whilst prepping your koftas, BOIL 200g - 250g roughly of uncooked rice.

- Add 125g of cooked white rice to your meal prep container with optional salad (I used cabbage lettuce tomato and cucumber).

ORANGE CHICKEN

Calories 340   **Carbs** 36g   **Protein** 32g   **Fat** 6g

Carbs mentioned are per meal. Store the meals in the fridge up to 3 days or keep it frozen up to 3 months

INGREDIENTS

600g raw diced chicken breast

200g roughly of uncooked rice

50ml of light soy sauce

200ml of low sugar orange juice

Tsp. soy sauce

Tbsp. garlic powder

20g cornflour

Tbsp. of olive oil

FOR THE ORANGE SAUCE

Tbsp. garlic paste

50ml light soy sauce

200ml low sugar orange juice

Drizzle of sriracha and honey

FULL RECIPE NEXT PAGE

Scan me !!

THE **ZACK CHUG** Cookbook

METHOD

- Add raw diced chicken breast in a bowl.

- Season with soy sauce, garlic powder, cornflour.
  (this makes it crispy)

- Mix it well together.

- Add olive oil to a pan and fry the chicken for 10-15 mins on medium to high heat golden brown and crispy (oven or air fry at 220°C for 15 mins until golden brown).

- Whilst prepping chicken, BOIL 200g - 250g roughly of uncooked rice.

FOR THE ORANGE SAUCE

- Add a tablespoon of garlic paste, light soy sauce, low sugar orange juice, drizzle of sriracha and honey.

- Add in your cooked chicken and optional to add sesame seeds and spring onions.

- Let it simmer for 5-10 mins until thick and sticky.

- Add equal amount of cooked chicken and 125g of cooked white rice to each meal prep containers.

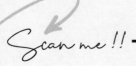

Scan me !!

ALFREDO FRIES

Calories 310   **Carbs** 28g   **Protein** 33g   **Fat** 6g

Carbs mentioned are per meal. Store the meals in the fridge up to 3 days or keep it frozen up to 3 months

INGREDIENTS

600g raw uncooked white potato

600g raw chicken breast

20g light butter

250ml skimmed milk (or milk of choice)

Tbsp. garlic powder

Tbsp. oregano

Tsp. paprika

Tsp. cornflour

Garlic

30g low fat cream cheese

20g low fat mozzarella cheese

Parsley & black pepper OPTIONAL

FULL RECIPE NEXT PAGE

THE ZACK CHUG Cookbook

Scan me !!

METHOD

- Slice raw potato.

- Season with garlic powder, oregano, paprika and cornflour to make the fries crispy.

- Mix it well together.

- Oven or air fry the fries at 220°C for 15 -20 mins mins until crispy and golden brown.

- Take a pan and, cook raw chicken breast (seasoned with garlic, oregano & paprika).

- Then set your chicken aside and add 20g light butter, garlic, skimmed milk, 30g low fat cream cheese, low fat mozzarella cheese.

- Add cooked chicken and parsley.

- Let it simmer on medium heat until rich and creamy.

- Optional to finish with black pepper.

- Add equal portions to each container.

THE
ZACK CHUG
Cookbook

HIGH PROTEIN MEAL PREP CHILLI GARLIC
FRIED RICE

Calories 340	**Carbs** 30g	**Protein** 32g	**Fat** 6g

Carbs mentioned are per meal. Store the meals in the fridge up to 3 days or keep it frozen up to 3 months

INGREDIENTS

Tsp. chilli flakes

Tbsp. garlic paste

80ml soy sauce

600g raw chicken breast

Drizzle of sriracha sauce

Low calorie oil spray

Tbsp. sesame oil

Garlic

Light soy sauce

Red bell pepper

220g of uncooked washed white rice

OPTIONAL spring onions and sesame seeds

FULL RECIPE NEXT PAGE

THE ZACK CHUG Cookbook

Scan me !!

METHOD

- To a bowl add a teaspoon chilli flakes, garlic paste, soy sauce, raw chicken breast, and a drizzle of sriracha sauce.

- Mix it well together.

- Pan fry on high heat for 10 mins using low calorie oil spray.

- Add the leftover sauce from cooking the chicken to a separate pan on medium heat and then add sesame oil, garlic, light soy sauce, red bell pepper, cooked rice and cooked chicken from before and stir well together.

- Top with optional spring onions and sesame seeds for that extra crunch.

- Add equal portions to each container.

THE
ZACK CHUG
Cookbook

Scan me !!

HIGH PROTEIN MEAL PREP CREAMY SPICY
PEANUT NOODLES

Calories 360	**Carbs** 33g	**Protein** 35g	**Fat** 10g

Carbs mentioned are per meal. Store the meals in the fridge up to 3 days or keep it frozen up to 3 months

FULL RECIPE NEXT PAGE

INGREDIENTS

600g raw chicken breast

Tsp. chilli powder

Tbsp. garlic powder

Sriracha sauce

50ml light soy sauce

Low calorie oil

Tbsp. sesame oil

Tbsp. minced garlic

Chilli flakes

Sesame seeds

30g peanut butter

80ml light soy sauce

Drizzle of honey

240g uncooked noodles

Spring onions

THE ZACK CHUG Cookbook

Scan me !!

METHOD

- Dice raw chicken breast and season with tsp. chilli powder, tbsp. garlic powder, sriracha sauce & 50ml light soy sauce.

- Mix it well together.

- Pan fry on high heat for 10 mins using low calorie oil spray (or air fry or oven @ 220 degrees).

- Then remove chicken and add to a pan add tbsp. sesame oil, minced garlic chilli flakes, sesame seeds, 30g peanut butter, light soy sauce and drizzle of honey.

- Add 750g cooked noodles (roughly 240g uncooked noodles).

- Your cooked chicken and finish with spring onions.

- Stir and let it simmer on low heat until rich and creamy.

HIGH PROTEIN MEAL PREP FLUFFY
CHICKEN BIRYANI

Calories 360	**Carbs** 38g	**Protein** 34g	**Fat** 6g

Carbs mentioned are per meal. Store the meals in the fridge up to 3 days or keep it frozen up to 3 months

FULL RECIPE NEXT PAGE

INGREDIENTS

600g raw chicken breast

150g low fat Greek yoghurt

Tbsp. paprika

Tsp. turmeric

Tsp. cinnamon

Low calorie oil spray

Tbsp. olive oil

Finely chopped onions

Tbsp. garlic paste

100g tomato purée

Tsp. garam masala

Tsp. cumin

220g of washed uncooked rice

OPTIONAL coriander and red chilli

THE
ZACK CHUG
C o o k b o o k

Scan me !!

METHOD

- Add diced chicken to a bowl.

- Marinade with 150g low fat Greek yoghurt, tablespoon paprika, tsp turmeric, teaspoon cinnamon.

- Mix it well together.

- Pan fry on high heat for 10 mins using low calorie oil spray (or air fry or oven @ 220 degrees).

- Then remove chicken and add to the same pan on medium heat olive oil, onions, garlic paste, tomato purée, garam masala and cumin.

- Whilst cooking chicken boil roughly 200g of washed uncooked rice.

- Add cooked chicken and 625g of cooked rice to the pan.

- Stir together and finish with optional coriander and red chilli.

- Add equal portions to each container.

THE
ZACK CHUG
Cookbook

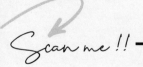

Scan me !!

CHICKEN

| **Calories** 330 | **Carbs** 38g | **Protein** 32g | **Fat** 7g |

Carbs mentioned are per meal. Store the meals in the fridge up to 3 days or keep it frozen up to 3 months

INGREDIENTS

600g raw chicken breast

Salt

Tsp. black pepper

50ml light soy sauce

20g cornflour

Tbsp. sesame oil

Minced garlic

Tsp. ginger

Chopped bell peppers & onions

60ml light soy sauce

Drizzle of honey

200g of washed uncooked rice

FULL RECIPE NEXT PAGE

Scan me !!

THE ZACK CHUG Cookbook

METHOD

- Add diced chicken to a bowl.

- Season with salt, teaspoon black pepper, light soy sauce & cornflour to make it crispy.

- Mix it well together & add to a pan with a tablespoon of sesame oil.

- Pan fry on high heat for 10 -15 mins until golden and crunchy.

- Then remove chicken and add to the same pan on medium heat minced garlic, teaspoon ginger, chopped bell peppers & onions.

- Add 60ml light soy sauce & drizzle of honey.

- Add cooked chicken.

- Stir well and top with optional spring onions.

- Whilst cooking chicken boil roughly 200g of washed uncooked rice.

- Add 125g or equal portions to each container.

THE ZACK CHUG Cookbook

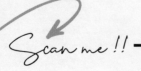

HIGH PROTEIN MEAL PREP CRISPY CHILLI
BEEF NOODLES

Calories	340	Carbs	32g	Protein	32g	Fat	9g

Carbs mentioned are per meal. Store the meals in the fridge up to 3 days or keep it frozen up to 3 months

INGREDIENTS

600g raw lean beef mince (or mince of choice)

Tbsp. garlic powder

Tbsp. paprika

Tsp. onion powder

Tbsp. olive oil

Garlic

Tsp. ginger

Tsp. chilli flakes

70ml light soy sauce

Drizzle of honey

Spring onions

240g uncooked noodles

OPTIONAL red chillis

FULL RECIPE NEXT PAGE

Scan me !!

THE ZACK CHUG Cookbook

METHOD

- Add lean beef mince (or mince of choice) to a bowl.

- Season with tablespoon garlic powder, tablespoon paprika and teaspoon of onion powder.

- Mix it well together.

- Add to a pan on high heat with a tablespoon of olive oil.

- Then add to the oil, garlic, ginger, chilli flakes.

- Add your raw mince and let it brown for 5 min.

- Add light soy sauce and drizzle of honey and let it simmer until crispy and sticky.

- Add spring onions followed by 750g cooked noodles (roughly 240g uncooked noodles).

- Stir together well and top with optional red chillis.

- Add equal portions to each container.

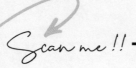

Scan me !!

THE ZACK CHUG Cookbook

FRIED RICE

Calories 330	**Carbs** 35g	**Protein** 32g	**Fat** 8g

Carbs mentioned are per meal. Store the meals in the fridge up to 3 days or keep it frozen up to 3 months

INGREDIENTS

600g raw diced chicken breast

Tbsp. garlic powder

Tsp. black pepper

50ml light soy sauce

Tsp. sesame oil

30g light butter

Chopped garlic

Frozen veg. of choice

220g of uncooked washed white rice

Sesame seeds

FULL RECIPE NEXT PAGE

THE ZACK CHUG Cookbook

Scan me !!

METHOD

- Add diced chicken breast to a bowl.

- Season with garlic powder, black pepper and 50ml light soy sauce & of sesame oil.

- Mix it well together & cook on a pan on high heat for 10-15 mins until golden brown and juicy or air fry or oven for 15 mins @ 220 °C.

- Then set your chicken aside and add to the pan light butter, chopped garlic, frozen veg of choice.

- Add 625g cooked rice (whilst chicken is cooking , boil 220g of uncooked washed white rice).

- Add cooked chicken.

- Stir it well together and let it simmer until it's crackling and finish with sesame seeds.

- Add equal portions to each container.

THE ZACK CHUG Cookbook

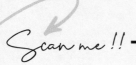 Scan me !!

BUFFALO TENDERS

Calories 310   **Carbs** 24g   **Protein** 31g   **Fat** 6g

Carbs mentioned are per meal. Store the meals in the fridge up to 3 days or keep it frozen up to 3 months

INGREDIENTS

600g raw diced chicken breast

600g raw potato sliced into fries

Tsp. chilli powder

Tbsp. oregano, garlic powder

Tsp. onion powder

30g cornflour

Olive oil

30g light butter

Hot sauce

Tbsp. bbq Sauce

Drizzle of honey

Parsley, garlic & oregano

FULL RECIPE NEXT PAGE

THE **ZACK CHUG** Cookbook

Scan me !!

METHOD

- Take 600g raw chicken breast and slice into tenders.

- Season with garlic powder, chilli powder, oregano & onion powder.

- Add cornflour to make it crispy.

- Mix and coat it well together & cook on a pan with a tablespoon of olive oil on high heat for 15-20 mins until golden brown and crunchy (or air fry or oven for 15 mins @ 220 °C).

- Then set your chicken aside and add to the pan light butter, hot sauce, bbq sauce & a drizzle of honey.

- Add your cooked chicken.

- Mix together and finish with parsley.

- Whilst chicken is cooking, air fry or oven 600g raw potato sliced into fries & seasoned with garlic and oregano, for 15 mins @ 220 °C.

- Add equal portions to each container.

THE
ZACK CHUG
Cookbook

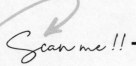

CHICKEN KORMA

Calories 380	**Carbs** 34g	**Protein** 32g	**Fat** 12g

Carbs mentioned are per meal. Store the meals in the fridge up to 3 days or keep it frozen up to 3 months

INGREDIENTS

600g raw chicken breast

Tbsp. olive oil, garlic powder & paprika

Tsp. garam masala

Chilli flakes

50g low fat Greek yoghurt

30g light butter

Tbsp. garlic paste

Ginger

200ml light coconut milk

40g low fat cream cheese

Pinch of turmeric

Coriander

200g of uncooked rice

FULL RECIPE NEXT PAGE

THE ZACK CHUG Cookbook

Scan me !!

METHOD

- Take 600g raw chicken breast and dice into cubes.

- Season with olive oil garlic powder, paprika, garam masala, chilli flakes & 50g low fat Greek yoghurt.

- Mix and coat it well together & cook on a pan on high heat for 15-20 mins until juicy and tender (or air fry or oven for 15 mins @ 220 °C).

- Then set your chicken aside and add to the pan light butter, garlic paste, ginger, light coconut milk, 40g low fat cream cheese.

- Add pinch of turmeric.

- Then add Your cooked chicken and stir well.

- Finish with coriander and let it simmer until rich and creamy.

- Whilst chicken is cooking, boil 200g of uncooked rice . (roughly equals 125g of cooked rice per meal)

- Add equal portions to each container.

THE ZACK CHUG Cookbook

PEPPER CHICKEN

Calories 320	**Carbs** 32g	**Protein** 32g	**Fat** 8g

Carbs mentioned are per meal. Store the meals in the fridge up to 3 days or keep it frozen up to 3 months

INGREDIENTS

600g raw chicken breast

Tbsp. garlic powder

Tbsp. oregano

Tsp. cumin

Black pepper

30g light butter

Garlic

Black pepper and lemon juice

Light soy sauce

Drizzle of honey

Parsley

200g of uncooked washed rice

FULL RECIPE NEXT PAGE

THE ZACK CHUG Cookbook

Scan me !!

METHOD

- Take 600g raw chicken breast and dice into cubes.

- Season with tablespoon garlic powder, tbsp. oregano & tsp. cumin & black pepper.

- Mix together & cook on a pan on high heat for 10-15 mins until sizzling brown(or air fry or oven for 15 mins @ 220 °C).

- Then set your chicken aside and on high heat add light butter, garlic, black pepper and lemon juice, light soy sauce.

- Add drizzle of honey.

- Add cooked chicken and Stir together and let it simmer for 10 mins on high heat until sticky.

- Finish with parsley.

- Meanwhile cook 200g of uncooked washed rice (will equal roughly 630g cooked rice).

- Add equal portions to each container.

THE ZACK CHUG Cookbook

RAMEN

Calories 340	**Carbs** 30g	**Protein** 34g	**Fat** 10g

Carbs mentioned are per meal. Store the meals in the fridge up to 3 days or keep it frozen up to 3 months

INGREDIENTS

600g raw chicken breast

Sriracha

30 ml light soy sauce

Tbsp. garlic powder

30g light butter

Tbsp. garlic paste

Tomato Paste

70ml light soy sauce

50ml water

30g low fat cream cheese

30g light cheddar cheese

240g uncooked noodles

FULL RECIPE NEXT PAGE

Scan me !!

THE **ZACK CHUG** Cookbook

METHOD

- Add diced raw chicken to a bowl.

- Season with sriracha, 30 ml light soy sauce and a tablespoon garlic powder.

- Mix together & cook on a pan on high heat for 10-15 mins until sizzling brown(or air fry or oven for 15 mins @ 220 °C).

- Then set your chicken aside and on medium heat add light butter, garlic paste, tomato paste, light soy sauce and water.

- Add low fat cream cheese and light cheddar.

- Simmer until the cheese sauce is thick then add cooked ramen noodles.

THE
ZACK CHUG
C o o k b o o k

GARLIC BEEF

Calories 320	**Carbs** 33g	**Protein** 32g	**Fat** 8g

Carbs mentioned are per meal. Store the meals in the fridge up to 3 days or keep it frozen up to 3 months

INGREDIENTS

600g raw lean beef

Tbsp. garlic powder

Tbsp. onion powder

Tbsp. chilli powder

Tbsp. sesame oil

Tbsp. garlic

Tsp. ginger

Chilli flakes

60ml light soy sauce

Sriracha

10g of honey

Spring onion

Sesame seeds

200g uncooked washed rice

FULL RECIPE NEXT PAGE

THE **ZACK CHUG** Cookbook

Scan me !!

METHOD

- Add raw lean beef to a bowl.

- Season with tablespoon garlic powder, tbsp. onion powder, chilli powder and chilli flakes.

- Add the seasoned beef to a pan.

- Cook for 10-15 mins until sizzling hot and brown.

- Then add light soy sauce, sriracha, honey, spring onion.

- Finish with sesame seeds.

- Whilst your beef is cooking, boil 200g uncooked washed rice (roughly is 630g cooked rice so roughly 125g cooked rice per container).

KUNG PAO CHICKEN

| **Calories** 340 | **Carbs** 35g | **Protein** 32g | **Fat** 6g |

Carbs mentioned are per meal. Store the meals in the fridge up to 3 days or keep it frozen up to 3 months

INGREDIENTS

600g raw chicken breast

Tbsp. garlic powder

30ml light soy sauce

Tbsp. sesame oil

Black pepper

Tbsp. garlic

Tsp. ginger

Bell pepper & spring onions

80ml light soy sauce

Tbsp. hoisin sauce

20g cornflour

10g of honey

5g crushed peanuts

200g uncooked washed

FULL RECIPE NEXT PAGE

Scan me !!

THE ZACK CHUG Cookbook

METHOD

- Dice raw chicken breast into pieces and add to a bowl.

- Season with tablespoon garlic powder, 30ml light soy sauce, sesame oil and black pepper.

- Mix together and cook on the pan on high heat for 10-15 mins until golden brown.

- Then on a pan on medium heat add garlic, ginger, bell pepper and spring onion.

- Add 80ml light soy sauce & tablespoon of hoisin sauce, cornflour & honey.

- Add your cooked chicken and let it simmer until thick.

- COMPLETELY OPTIONAL to add 5g crushed peanuts.

- Whilst your chicken is cooking, boil 200g uncooked washed rice.
  (roughly is 630g cooked rice so roughly 125g cooked rice per container)

THE ZACK CHUG Cookbook

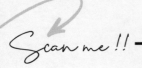

Scan me !!

HABANERO CHICKEN

| **Calories** 340 | **Carbs** 34g | **Protein** 32g | **Fat** 8g |

Carbs mentioned are per meal. Store the meals in the fridge up to 3 days or keep it frozen up to 3 months

INGREDIENTS

600g raw chicken breast

Tbsp. garlic powder

Tbsp. oregano

Tsp. chilli powder

Tbsp. olive oil

30g light butter

Tbsp. garlic

70ml hot sauce

200ml low sugar mango juice

10g honey

Coriander

200g uncooked washed rice

FULL RECIPE NEXT PAGE

THE **ZACK CHUG** Cookbook

Scan me !!

METHOD

- Dice the raw chicken breast into pieces.

- Season with tablespoon garlic powder, oregano, chilli powder and olive oil.

- Mix together and cook on the pan on high heat for 10-15 mins until sizzling brown (or can air fry or oven for 15 mins @ 220 degrees).

- Then remove the chicken and add light butter, tablespoon garlic, hot sauce, low sugar mango juice and honey.

- Add cooked chicken and mix it all together.

- Let it simmer for 5-10 mins on high heat until sticky and thick.

- Finish with coriander.

- Whilst your chicken is cooking, boil 200g uncooked washed rice.
  (roughly is 630g cooked rice so roughly 125g cooked rice per container)

THE
ZACK CHUG
C o o k b o o k

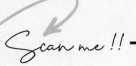

HIGH PROTEIN MEAL PREP CREAMY LEMON
GARLIC PASTA

Calories 380	Carbs 36g	Protein 36g	Fat 9g

Carbs mentioned are per meal. Store the meals in the fridge up to 3 days or keep it frozen up to 3 months

INGREDIENTS

600g raw chicken breast

Tbsp. garlic powder

Tbsp. oregano

Tbsp. paprika

Tbsp. olive oil

250g uncooked pasta

30g light butter

Tbsp. garlic

Lemon juice

Parsley

250ml pasta water

70g low fat cream cheese

20g parmesan cheese

FULL RECIPE NEXT PAGE

Scan me !!

165

THE ZACK CHUG Cookbook

METHOD

- Take raw chicken breast and season with tablespoon garlic powder, oregano, paprika and olive oil.

- Mix together and air fry or oven for 15 mins @ 220 °C
(or cook on the pan on high heat for 10-15 mins until sizzling brown) .

- Slice the chicken into strips.

- Meanwhile boil 250g of uncooked pasta for 15 mins.

- Then on medium heat to a pan add light butter, garlic, lemon juice & parsley.

- Also add pasta water , low fat cream cheese and parmesan cheese.

- Add cooked pasta to the pan.

- Stir and mix it well until thick and creamy.

- Add your chicken on top of the pasta and finish with leftover pasta sauce from the pan.

- Add roughly 120-130g of cooked pasta to each container.

THE ZACK CHUG Cookbook

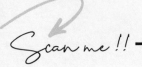

Scan me !!

BIG MAC BURGER

| **Calories** 380 | **Carbs** 31g | **Protein** 38g | **Fat** 11g |

Carbs mentioned are per meal. Store the meals in the fridge up to 3 days or keep it frozen up to 3 months

FULL RECIPE NEXT PAGE

INGREDIENTS

600g raw lean beef

Tbsp. garlic powder

Tbsp. paprika

Tbsp. onion powder

Tbsp. olive oil

50g low fat Greek yoghurt

Tbsp. light ketchup

Mustard (to taste preference)

Chopped gherkins

OPTIONAL lettuce

Toasted brioche buns

THE ZACK CHUG Cookbook

Scan me !!

METHOD

- Take 600g raw lean beef.

- Season with tablespoon garlic powder, tbsp. paprika, tbsp. onion powder and a tbsp. olive oil.

- Mix together and form equal balls and smash each ball into a burger patty.

- Pan fry each patty on high heat for 2-3 mins on each side.

- Add a light cheese slice to each patty and let it melt.

- Double stack each patty, you should form 5 double stacks.

FOR THE HEALTHY BIG MAC BURGER SAUCE

- Add low fat Greek yoghurt , light ketchup and mustard to taste preference.

- Add chopped gherkins and mix well.

- Assemble the patties with the sauce, optional lettuce, gherkins and toasted brioche buns.

- Tightly seal with foil to store and DIG IN.

THE **ZACK CHUG** Cookbook

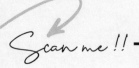

Scan me !!

SWEET & SOUR CHICKEN

Calories 330	**Carbs** 33g	**Protein** 32g	**Fat** 5g

Carbs mentioned are per meal. Store the meals in the fridge up to 3 days or keep it frozen up to 3 months

INGREDIENTS

600g raw chicken breast

Tbsp. light soy sauce

Tbsp. olive oil

Tbsp. garlic powder

30g cornflour

Tbsp. garlic paste

Chopped bell peppers and onions

80ml light soy sauce

Tbsp. ketchup

200ml low sugar orange juice

10g of honey

OPTIONAL spring onions

200g uncooked washed white

FULL RECIPE NEXT PAGE

THE **ZACK CHUG** Cookbook

Scan me !!

METHOD

- Dice 600g raw chicken breast.

- Season with tablespoon light soy sauce, tbsp. garlic powder and 30g cornflour to make it crispy.

- Mix together and coat the chicken well.

- Add to a pan with a tablespoon of olive oil and cook for 10-15 mins on high heat until golden and crunchy.

- Set chicken aside and add tablespoon of garlic paste, chopped bell-peppers and onions, light soy sauce, ketchup, low sugar orange juice and honey.

- Add crispy cooked chicken to the pan.

- Stir it all together and simmer on medium heat.

- Finish with optional spring onions.

- Whilst your chicken is cooking, boil 200g uncooked washed white rice (roughly 630g of cooked rice, portion equally per container)

- Add 125g or equal portions to each container .

POPCORN CHICKEN

| **Calories** 500 | **Carbs** 20g | **Protein** 85g | **Fat** 8g |

Carbs mentioned are per meal.

INGREDIENTS

400g raw chicken breast

2 Tbsp. garlic powder

50ml hot sauce

3 rice cakes

Tbsp. paprika

Tbsp. oregano

Parsley

FULL RECIPE NEXT PAGE

THE ZACK CHUG Cookbook

Scan me !!

METHOD

- Slice raw chicken breast into cubes.

- Season with tablespoon garlic powder & 50ml hot sauce and mix well.

- Then blend 3 rice cakes with tbsp. garlic powder, paprika & oregano.

- Dip and coat your cubed chicken into the fine rice cake powder.

- Oven or air fry for 10-15 mins @ 220°C until nice and crispy.

- Finish with parsley and enjoy.

THE
ZACK CHUG
Cookbook

Scan me !!

SANDWICH

Calories 550	**Carbs** 40g	**Protein** 63g	**Fat** 8g

Carbs mentioned are per sandwich. The measurements used in this recipe is for one sandwich.

INGREDIENTS

250g raw chicken breast

Tbsp. garlic powder

10g sriracha sauce

50g egg whites

25g cornflakes

Tbsp. garlic powder

Tbsp. black pepper

Tbsp. oregano

Light brioche bun

GARLIC MAYO SAUCE :

Tbsp. light mayo

Garlic paste

Lemon juice

Black pepper

Lettuce

FULL RECIPE NEXT PAGE

THE **ZACK CHUG** Cookbook

Scan me !!

METHOD

- Take 250g raw chicken breast

- Season with tbsp. garlic powder & sriracha sauce & egg whites and mix well.

- Then blend cornflakes with tablespoon of garlic powder, tbsp. black pepper & tbsp. oregano.

- Dip and coat your chicken into the fine cornflake coating powder.

- Oven or air fry for 10-15 mins @ 220°C until golden brown and crispy.

FOR THE GARLIC MAYO SAUCE

- Add light mayo, garlic paste (to taste preference), lemon juice and black pepper to a bowl and mix well.

- Assemble the sandwich with a light brioche bun & lettuce.

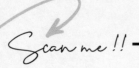

HIGH PROTEIN MEAL PREP CHILLI GARLIC
PASTA

Calories 330	**Carbs** 37g	**Protein** 34g	**Fat** 5g

Carbs mentioned are per meal. Store the meals in the fridge up to 3 days or keep it frozen up to 3 months

INGREDIENTS

Garlic

Tbsp. chilli flakes

600g raw diced chicken breast

20g sriracha

250g of uncooked pasta

200ml pasta water

Tbsp. olive oil

Tbsp. garlic paste

Tbsp. chilli flakes

20g sriracha

parsley

FULL RECIPE NEXT PAGE

Scan me !!

THE **ZACK CHUG** Cookbook

METHOD

- Add garlic, tablespoon chilli flakes, raw diced chicken breast & 20g sriracha to a bowl.

- Mix well and cook on a pan for 10-15 mins on high heat.

- Meanwhile boil 250g of uncooked pasta and save 200-300ml pasta water from it.

- On medium heat to a pan add tablespoon of olive oil, tablespoon of garlic paste, tablespoon chilli flakes, 20g sriracha, pasta water and then let it simmer.

- Add your cooked pasta and chicken and stir together.

- Finish with optional parsley.

- Add roughly 120-130g cooked pasta to each container.

THE
ZACK CHUG
Cookbook

HOT TENDERS

Calories 560	Carbs 30g	Protein 90g	Fat 8g

Carbs mentioned are per meal.

INGREDIENTS

400g raw chicken breast

Tbsp. garlic powder

Tbsp. paprika

80ml hot sauce

35g cornflakes

Tbsp. oregano

Parsley

FULL RECIPE NEXT PAGE

THE ZACK CHUG Cookbook

Scan me !!

METHOD

- Take 400g raw chicken breast and slice into strips.

- Season with tablespoon garlic powder, tablespoon paprika & 80ml hot sauce.

- Mix all well.

- Then crush 35g cornflakes and season with tablespoon of garlic powder, tbsp. paprika & tbsp. oregano.

- Dip and coat your chicken into the cornflakes.

- Oven or air fry for 10-15 mins @ 220°C until nice crispy and golden.

- Finish with some hot sauce on top and parsley.

THE
ZACK CHUG
Cookbook

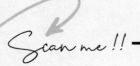
Scan me !!

HIGH PROTEIN TACO BELL CHEESY CHICKEN
QUESADILLA

Calories 590	**Carbs** 39g	**Protein** 53g	**Fat** 20g

Carbs mentioned are per meal.

INGREDIENTS

200g raw cubed chicken breast

Tsp. chilli powder

Tbsp. garlic powder

Oregano

Tsp cumin & tsp. olive oil

FOR THE CREAMY SAUCE:

30g light mayo

Jalapeños and jalapeño juice

Tsp. paprika

Tsp. garlic powder

2 light low cal tortilla wrap

15g light mozzarella

15g light cheddar cheese

FULL RECIPE NEXT PAGE

Scan me !!

METHOD

- Get 200g raw cubed chicken breast and season with tsp. chilli powder tablespoon garlic powder, tablespoon oregano, tsp cumin & tsp. olive oil.

- Mix well and cook on the pan on high heat for 10 mins (or oven or air fry for 10-15 mins @ 220°C until juicy and golden).

FOR THE CREAMY SAUCE

- Add light mayo, jalapeños and jalapeño juice, tsp. paprika and tsp. garlic powder and mix until thick.

- Then to a pan add light low cal tortilla wrap, 15g of light mozzarella & 15g light cheddar cheese.

- Add Your cooked chicken and creamy sauce.

- Add another low cal wrap on top.

- Heat for 2-3 mins on high heat on each side until crispy.

- Finish with coriander and cut into equal slices.

THE **ZACK CHUG** Cookbook

Scan me !!

HIGH PROTEIN STUFFED
GARLIC FLATBREAD

Calories 550   **Carbs** 48g   **Protein** 40g   **Fat** 15g

Carbs mentioned are per meal.

INGREDIENTS

100g raw chicken breast

Tbsp. oregano

Tbsp. garlic powder

Tsp. cumin

Tsp. olive oil

Low cal oil spray

Tbsp. garlic paste

FOR THE FLATBREAD BASE :

70g Self raising flour

79g low fat Greek yoghurt

Tbsp. garlic paste

Parsley

20g mozzarella cheese

5g light butter

FULL RECIPE NEXT PAGE

THE **ZACK CHUG** Cookbook

Scan me !!

METHOD

- Take raw chicken breast and cut into pieces

- Season with tbsp oregano, garlic powder , cumin and tsp olive oil and mix well.

- Pan fry using low cal oil spray for 10 mins on high heat.
  (or oven or Air fry for 10-15 mins @ 220°C)

FOR THE FLATBREAD BASE

- Take self raising flour and low fat Greek yoghurt and mix into a ball on a floured surface and flatten.

- Add tbsp garlic paste in the middle with parsley, your cooked chicken and mozzarella cheese.

- Fold the edges and flatten again.

- High Heat for 2 mins on each side of the flat bread.

- Then add 5g light butter and a tablespoon of garlic paste and let it melt.

- Cut in half and you're all done!

Scan me !!

THE
ZACK CHUG
Cookbook

MCNUGGETS

| **Calories** 470 | **Carbs** 17g | **Protein** 74g | **Fat** 10g |

Carbs mentioned are per meal.

INGREDIENTS

300g raw chicken breast

Tbsp. paprika

2 Tbsp. garlic

Black pepper

Egg

OPTIONAL Salt and Ketchup

FOR THE COATING:

3 rice cakes

Tbsp. garlic

Tbsp. paprika

Tsp. black pepper

Low calorie oil spray

FULL RECIPE NEXT PAGE

THE **ZACK CHUG** Cookbook

Scan me !!

METHOD

- Take raw chicken breast and mince it with a knife or use a blender.

- Season with tbsp. garlic, tbsp. paprika, black pepper and one egg.

- Mix well and roll into nuggets.

For the COATING

- Add 3 rice cakes, tbsp garlic, tbsp paprika, and tsp black pepper to a blender and make a fine powder.

- Dip and coat your chicken well in the powder.

- Oven or air fry for 10-15 mins @ 220°C using low cal oil spray.

- Optional to finish with salt and enjoy with ketchup.

THE
ZACK CHUG
Cookbook

Scan me !!

CHICKEN GYOZAS

| **Calories** 590 | **Carbs** 55g | **Protein** 52g | **Fat** 12g |

Carbs mentioned are per meal.

INGREDIENTS

175g raw chicken breast

Tbsp. paprika

2 Tbsp. garlic

Tbsp. light soy sauce

Black pepper

Chopped spring onions

OPTIONAL chilli soy sauce

FOR THE GYOZA BASE :

80g self raising flour

80g low fat Greek yoghurt

Tsp. olive oil

FULL RECIPE NEXT PAGE

THE
ZACK CHUG
Cookbook

Scan me !!

METHOD

- Take raw chicken breast and mince it with a knife or use a blender.

- Season with tablespoon garlic, black pepper, tbsp. light soy sauce and chopped spring onions.

- Mix well

FOR THE GYOZA BASE

- Take self raising flour & low fat Greek yoghurt and mix it well together.

- Knead on a floured surface into a ball.

- Flatten out and make into circles with a cup, use excess dough and flatten out again into more circles

- Add the chicken mix and fold and pinch the edges.

- Add the gyozas a pan with a tsp. olive oil and heat for 5 mins on high heat add a drop of water and let it steam for 2 mins until soft and smooth.

- Enjoy with optional chilli soy sauce.

THE
ZACK CHUG
Cookbook

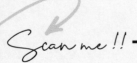

HIGH PROTEIN PULLED
CHICKEN TACOS

| **Calories** 590 | **Carbs** 42g | **Protein** 52g | **Fat** 17g |

Carbs mentioned are for all.

INGREDIENTS

200g raw chicken breast

3 low cal small tortilla

30g mozzarella cheese

2 Tbsp. paprika

2 Tbsp. garlic powder

2 Tsp. cumin and Tsp. olive oil

Low cal oil spray

Chopped bell peppers, onions & black pepper

Chopped tomato tin

OPTIONAL guacamole or salsa

Coriander

FULL RECIPE NEXT PAGE

THE ZACK CHUG Cookbook

Scan me !!

METHOD

- Take chicken breast and season with tablespoon paprika, tbsp. garlic powder , tsp cumin and tsp olive oil.

- Mix it all well.

- Pan fry using low cal oil spray for 10-15 mins on high heat.
  (or oven / air fry 15 mins @ 220 degrees)

- Shred the cooked chicken.

- Then on medium heat to a pan add chopped bell peppers & onions.

- Add same seasonings as used before on chicken.

- Add a chopped tomato tin and shredded chicken and coriander.

- Dip your low cal small tortilla into the mix and add to pan with your taco mix and 10g mozzarella cheese per wrap.
  (30g mozzarella cheese used all together)

- Heat for 2 mins on each side until crispy and cheesy.

- Enjoy with optional guacamole or salsa.

THE
ZACK CHUG
Cookbook

Scan me !!

BAO BUNS

Calories 550	**Carbs** 60g	**Protein** 47g	**Fat** 10g

Carbs mentioned are for all.

INGREDIENTS

150g raw chicken breast

Tbsp. garlic powder

15g sriracha

Black pepper

Tsp. soy sauce

10g of honey

10g hot sauce

5g of sesame seeds

FOR THE BAO BUNS

89g self raising flour

80g low fat Greek yoghurt

20ml water

OPTIONAL spring onions

FULL RECIPE NEXT PAGE

THE ZACK CHUG Cookbook

Scan me !!

METHOD

- Take 150g raw chicken breast and cut into pieces.

- Season it with tablespoon garlic powder, 15g sriracha, black pepper and tsp soy sauce.

- Mix well and oven / air fry 15 mins @ 220 degrees.
  (I used an air fryer, they came out crispy)

- Coat the chicken with 10g of honey and hot sauce mixed together and 5g of sesame seeds.

FOR THE BAO BUNS

- Mix together 89g self raising flour & 80g low fat Greek yoghurt and knead on a floured surface into a ball.

- Flatten and make circles with a cup, then fold each circle over.

- Add to pan on medium to high heat with 20ml water.

- Let it steam for 10-15 mins whilst adding drops of water in between steaming.

- Finish with optional spring onions.

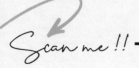

LOADED FRIES

| **Calories** 690 | **Carbs** 65g | **Protein** 68g | **Fat** 17g |

INGREDIENTS

300g raw uncooked potato

2 Tbsp. garlic powder

2 Tbsp. oregano

2 Tbsp. paprika

Chopped onions

250g raw lean beef mince

Chopped tomato tin

30g mozzarella cheese

FOR THE BIG MAC SAUCE :

30g light mayo

Tbsp. ketchup

Tbsp. mustard

Gherkins

Parsley

FULL RECIPE NEXT PAGE

THE **ZACK CHUG** Cookbook

Scan me !!

METHOD

- Slice 300g raw uncooked potato into french fries.

- Season with tbsp garlic powder, tbsp oregano & tbsp paprika.

- Mix well and oven or air fry for 15 mins @ 220°C until crispy.

- Then on medium heat add to a pan chopped onions and tomato tin, beef mince, mozzarella cheese and tbsp of same seasonings used on potato.

- Let it simmer for 5-10 mins until cheesy.

FOR THE BIG MAC SAUCE

- Mix together light mayo, tbsp. ketchup & mustard, gherkins.

- Load it all on top of each other and dig in.

- Finish with parsley.

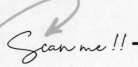

Scan me !!

THE ZACK CHUG Cookbook

HIGH PROTEIN CHICKEN
GYROS & GARLIC NAAN

Calories 480	**Carbs** 45g	**Protein** 60g	**Fat** 17g

INGREDIENTS

200g raw chicken breast

75g low fat Greek yoghurt

Tbsp. garlic

Tsp. olive oil

Tbsp. paprika & cumin

Lemon juice

OPTIONAL skewers

FOR THE GARLIC NAAN

50g self raising flour

60g low fat greek yoghurt

Tbsp. garlic powder

FOR THE TZATZIKI SAUCE

50g low fat Greek yoghurt

Chopped cucumber

Tsp. mint sauce & garlic paste

FULL RECIPE NEXT PAGE

THE ZACK CHUG Cookbook

Scan me !!

METHOD

- Thinly slice raw chicken breast and season with low fat Greek yoghurt, tbsp garlic, tsp olive oil, tbsp paprika and tbsp. cumin and lemon juice.

- Mix well and OPTIONAL to add to skewers with an onion as the base.

- Oven or air fry for 15-20 mins @ 220°C.

FOR THE GARLIC NAAN

- Mix together self raising flour, 60g low fat Greek yoghurt and tbsp garlic powder.

- Knead on a floured surface into a ball and flatten out.

- High heat on the pan for 2-3 mins on each side.

FOR THE TZATZIKI SAUCE

- Add 50g low fat Greek yoghurt , chopped cucumber, tsp mint sauce and tsp. garlic paste.

- Mix it all well.

- Assemble all and top it off with optional salad of choice.

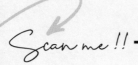

KOREAN FRIED CHICKEN

Calories 350	**Carbs** 36g	**Protein** 32g	**Fat** 8g

Carbs mentioned are per meal.

FULL RECIPE NEXT PAGE

INGREDIENTS

600g raw diced chicken breast

Tbsp. of soy sauce

Tbsp. garlic powder

30g of corn flour

Tbsp. olive oil

30g light butter

Tbsp. garlic

40g tomato paste

Sriracha sauce

100ml light soy sauce

10g honey

OPTIONAL sesame seeds

200g uncooked rice

THE ZACK CHUG Cookbook

Scan me !!

METHOD

- Season chicken breast with tbsp. of soy sauce, tablespoon of garlic powder, and cornflour (this makes it crispy)

- Mix it well together.

- Add a tablespoon of olive oil to a pan and fry the chicken for 10-15 mins on medium to high heat golden brown and crispy.
  (or oven or air fry at 220°C for 15 mins until golden brown)

FOR THE STICKY SAUCE

- Add 30g light butter, tbsp garlic, tomato paste, sriracha sauce, 10g honey and 100ml light soy sauce .
  (add water if you want more volume to your sauce)

- Add cooked chicken and let it simmer for 5-10 mins until thick and sticky.

- Optional to add sesame seeds.

- Whilst prepping chicken, BOIL 200g roughly of uncooked rice.

- Add roughly 125g of cooked white rice to each container.

THE ZACK CHUG Cookbook

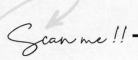

CHICKEN PASTA

Calories 380	**Carbs** 40g	**Protein** 36g	**Fat** 8g

Fridge up to 3 days or Freeze up to 3 months and 2-3 Mins microwave for Reheating

FULL RECIPE NEXT PAGE

INGREDIENTS

600g raw chicken breast

2 Tbsp. chilli powder

2 Tbsp. oregano

2 Tbsp. garlic Powder

2 Tbsp. coriander

70ml hot sauce

30g light butter

Tbsp. garlic

Chopped onion

150g tomato pasata sauce

50g hot sauce

40g low fat cream cheese

200g -250g uncooked pasta

40g mozzarella cheese

Parsley

THE ZACK CHUG Cookbook

Scan me !!

METHOD

- Season chicken breast with tbsp. chilli powder, tbsp. oregano. tbsp. garlic powder, tbsp. coriander and 70ml hot sauce .
(I used Nando's hot sauce but any hot sauce is fine too)

- Mix it all together & cook for 15 mins on medium heat on a pan, set the chicken aside and then to the same pan add 30g light butter, tbsp. garlic & chopped onion.

- Add tomato sauce and same seasonings as used in chicken
(chilli, oregano, garlic and coriander)

- Add 50g hot sauce, 40g low fat cream cheese, already boiled pasta.
(boil while prepping the chicken)

- Add 40g mozzarella cheese and stir together.

- Add the cooked chicken and parsley and simmer until it's all nice and creamy.

- Make equal portions in your meal prep containers.

THE ZACK CHUG Cookbook

PARMESAN TENDERS

Calories 570	**Carbs** 19g	**Protein** 70g	**Fat** 13g

Carbs mentioned are per meal.

FULL RECIPE NEXT PAGE

INGREDIENTS

250g raw chicken breast

Tbsp. garlic

Tbsp. paprika

Black pepper

1 egg

FOR THE COATING

3 rice cakes

10g parmesan cheese

Tbsp. garlic

Tbsp. paprika

Tbsp. oregano

Low cal oil spray

FOR THE BUTTER GARLIC SAUCE

30g light butter

Parsley

Tbsp. garlic paste

10g parmesan cheese

THE ZACK CHUG Cookbook

Scan me !!

METHOD

- Take raw chicken breast and mince it with a knife or use a blender.

- Season with tablespoon garlic, tbsp paprika, black pepper and one egg.

- Mix well and roll and flatten into tenders.

FOR THE COATING

- Add 3 rice cakes, 10g parmesan cheese, tbsp. garlic, tbsp paprika, tbsp oregano in a blender.

- Blend it into fine powder and dip and coat your chicken well.

- Oven or air fry for 10-15 mins at 220°C using low cal oil spray.

FOR THE BUTTER GARLIC SAUCE

- On medium heat add 30g light butter, parsley, tbsp garlic paste, 10g parmesan cheese.

- Mix and add to the tenders.

- Optional to enjoy with buffalo sauce.

HIGH PROTEIN CHICKEN
DOUGHNUTS

Calories 490   **Carbs** 23g   **Protein** 74g   **Fat** 10g

Carbs mentioned are for all.

FULL RECIPE NEXT PAGE

INGREDIENTS

300g raw chicken breast

Tbsp. garlic

Tbsp. paprika

Tbsp. black pepper

Coriander

1 egg

Low cal oil spray

Parsley (OPTIONAL)

FOR THE COATING:

30g cornflakes

Tsp. garlic

Black pepper

Tsp. paprika

Scan me !!

METHOD

- Take 300g raw chicken breast and mince it with blender or using 2 knives.

- Season with tablespoon garlic, tbsp paprika, black pepper and coriander and one egg.

- Mix it all well, roll and poke a hole in the middle.

FOR THE COATING

- Take cornflakes, tsp garlic, black pepper, tsp paprika and mix together.

- Dip and coat your chicken well.

- Oven or air fry for 10-15 mins @ 220°C using low cal oil spray.

- Optional to finish with parsley and enjoy with light garlic mayo.

THE ZACK CHUG Cookbook

CHICKEN BURRITOS

Calories 420	**Carbs** 40g	**Protein** 36g	**Fat** 11g

Carbs mentioned are per meal.

Fridge up to 3 days or Freeze up to 3 months and 2-3 Mins microwave for Reheating

FULL RECIPE NEXT PAGE

INGREDIENTS

600g raw chicken breast

Garlic

Tbsp. cumin & paprika

Lime juice

15g sriracha

Tsp. olive oil

60g sweetcorn

Coriander

80ml hot sauce

60g low fat cream cheese

25g mozzarella cheese

250g cooked rice

5 low cal tortilla wraps

THE **ZACK CHUG** Cookbook

Scan me !!

METHOD

- Dice raw chicken breast.

- Season with garlic, tbsp. cumin, tbsp paprika, lime juice, 15g sriracha & tsp olive oil.

- Mix it well together.

- Pan fry the chicken for 10-15 mins on medium to high heat golden brown and crispy (or oven or air fry at 220°C for 15 mins until golden brown)

- Then add sweetcorn, coriander, hot sauce, low fat cream cheese and 25g mozzarella cheese.

- Stir and add 250g cooked rice.

- Simmer on low heat for 5 mins until creamy.

- Add equal portions to 5 low cal tortilla wraps and wrap it up and tightly seal with foil.

THE
ZACK CHUG
Cookbook

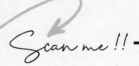

Scan me !!

HIGH PROTEIN MEAL CREAMY SESAME
CHICKEN RAMEN

Calories 360	**Carbs** 37g	**Protein** 35g	**Fat** 5g

Carbs mentioned are per meal. Fridge up to 3 days or Freeze up to 3 months .

INGREDIENTS

600g raw chicken breast

Garlic & black pepper

Tbsp. onion powder

30ml light soy sauce

10g sesame oil

Spring onion

20g sriracha

10g sesame seed

10g honey

60ml light soy sauce

600g cooked ramen

60g low fat cream cheese

FULL RECIPE NEXT PAGE

Scan me !!

205

METHOD

- Take 600g raw chicken breast and dice into cubes.

- Season with garlic, black pepper, tbsp onion powder, 30ml light soy sauce and 10g sesame oil.

- Mix together & cook on a pan on high heat for 10-15 mins until sizzling brown (or air fry or oven for 15 mins @ 220 °C).

- Then on medium heat add spring onion, sriracha, sesame seed, honey, light soy sauce, 600g cooked ramen and low fat cream cheese.

- Stir and let it simmer on low heat until rich and creamy.

- Add equal portions to your prep containers.

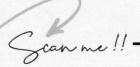

THE ZACK CHUG Cookbook

HIGH PROTEIN MEAL STICKY HONEY
GARLIC CHICKEN

Calories 310	**Carbs** 36g	**Protein** 32g	**Fat** 6g

Carbs mentioned are per meal. Fridge up to 3 days or Freeze up to 3 months .

INGREDIENTS

600g raw chicken breast

Tbsp garlic, paprika

Tsp. cumin

30ml light soy sauce

Chilli flakes

30 light butter

Tbsp. garlic

40ml light soy sauce

10g honey

10g sesame seeds

200g uncooked rice

FULL RECIPE NEXT PAGE

Scan me !!

THE ZACK CHUG Cookbook

METHOD

- Get 600g raw chicken breast and season with tbsp garlic, tbsp paprika, tsp. cumin, 30ml light soy sauce and chilli flakes.

- Mix together & on medium heat to a pan add 30 light butter and tbsp garlic.

- Cook 10-15 mins until a buttery sauce forms and then add 40ml light soy sauce and 10g honey.

- Simmer for 5 mins and add 10g sesame seeds.

- Meanwhile boil 200g uncooked rice (will equal roughly 630g cooked rice)

- Add equal portions to your prep containers.

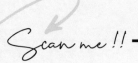

THE
ZACK CHUG
Cookbook

HIGH PROTEIN MEAL HONEY BBQ
MAC N CHEESE

Calories 380	**Carbs** 37g	**Protein** 36g	**Fat** 9g

Carbs mentioned are per meal. Fridge up to 3 days or Freeze up to 3 months .

INGREDIENTS

600g raw chicken breast

Tbsp. black pepper, garlic & paprika

Tsp. olive oil

50g bbq sauce

10g honey

Parsley

MAC N CHEESE:

30g light butter

80ml hot sauce

60g low fat cream cheese

20g cheddar cheese

500g cooked macaroni pasta

10g sesame seeds

FULL RECIPE NEXT PAGE

Scan me !!

THE ZACK CHUG Cookbook

METHOD

- Get 600g raw chicken breast and dice it.

- Season with black pepper, tbsp garlic, tbsp paprika, tsp. olive oil.

- Mix together & cook on high heat on a pan for 10 mins.

- Then add 50g bbq sauce, 10g honey , parsley and stir together.

- For the mac n cheese on medium heat add light butter, hot sauce, low fat cream cheese and 20g cheddar cheese.

- Add cooked macaroni pasta.

- Stir together until nice and creamy.

- Simmer for 5 mins and add 10g sesame seeds.

- Add equal portions to your prep containers.

THE ZACK CHUG Cookbook

FRIED CHICKEN

Calories 330	**Carbs** 38g	**Protein** 32g	**Fat** 4g

Carbs mentioned are per meal. Fridge up to 3 days or Freeze up to 3 months .

INGREDIENTS

600g raw chicken breast

Tbsp. oregano

Tbsp. garlic powder &
onion powder

Tbsp. paprika

30g corn flour

50ml Worcestershire
sauce

10g honey

Parsley

200g of uncooked rice

METHOD

- Get 600g raw chicken breast and dice.

- Season with tbsp oregano, tbsp garlic powder, tbsp onion powder, tbsp paprika and corn flour to make it crispy.

Continued...

- Mix together & optional to coat using a seal zip lock bag.

- Cook on high heat on a pan for 10 -15 mins.

- Then add Worcestershire sauce, honey & parsley.

- Simmer and stir together.

- Meanwhile cook 200g of uncooked washed rice (will equal roughly 630g cooked rice).

- Add equally to meal prep containers.

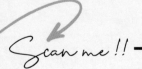

THE ZACK CHUG Cookbook

HIGH PROTEIN MEAL PREP ORANGE CHICKEN
BURRITOS

Calories 380   **Carbs** 45g   **Protein** 33g   **Fat** 7g

Carbs mentioned are per BURRITO. Fridge up to 3 days or Freeze up to 3 months .

FULL RECIPE NEXT PAGE

INGREDIENTS

600g raw chicken breast

Tbsp. garlic powder

30ml light soy sauce

Tbsp. paprika

Tsp. sesame oil & ginger

Tbsp. garlic paste

150ml low sugar orange juice

50ml light soy sauce

15g honey

15g sriracha

5g cornflour

50ml water

5 low cal tortilla wrap

350g cooked rice

Spring onion

THE ZACK CHUG Cookbook

Scan me !!

METHOD

- Get 600g raw chicken breast and dice.

- Season with tbsp garlic powder, 30ml light soy sauce, tbsp paprika, tsp sesame oil.

- Mix it all together.

- Cook on high heat on a pan for 10 -15 mins until sizzling.

- Set chicken aside then add on medium heat tbsp garlic paste, ginger, low sugar orange juice, light soy sauce, 15g honey and 15g sriracha.

- Add 5g cornflour mixed with 50ml of water.

- Then add cooked chicken and let it simmer and thicken together.

- Finish with sesame seeds.

FOR THE BURRITO ASSEMBLY

- Get 5 low cal tortilla wrap.

- Add 70g cooked rice per wrap (350g cooked rice all together).

- Then add equal servings of your orange chicken and spring onion.

- Roll it up, optional to grill and tightly seal with foil.

CHEESE FRIES

| **Calories** 360 | **Carbs** 22g | **Protein** 34g | **Fat** 11g |

Carbs mentioned are per meal. Fridge up to 3 days or Freeze up to 3 months .

INGREDIENTS

600g raw white potato

2 Tbsp. oregano, garlic powder & chilli powder

Tsp. olive oil

600g lean beef mince

Tbsp. tomato paste

80ml hot sauce

60g low fat cream cheese

30g cheddar cheese

Spring onion

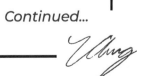

METHOD

- Take raw uncooked white potato and season with tbsp oregano, tbsp garlic powder tbsp chilli powder & tsp olive oil.

- Mix together and oven or air fry for 15-20@ 220°C.

- Then on medium heat, add lean beef mince same seasonings used on fries (tbsp oregano, garlic and chilli powder).

Continued...

Scan me !!

- Add tbsp tomato paste, hot sauce and low fat cream cheese.

- Mix all together.

- Add 30g cheddar cheese and let it simmer and melt for 5 mins.

- Finish off with spring onion.

- Add equal portions of fries and beef mince to your meal prep containers and OPTIONAL to finish with red chillis.

THE
ZACK CHUG
Cookbook

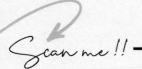

CHILLI CHICKEN

| **Calories** 350 | **Carbs** 38g | **Protein** 32g | **Fat** 6g |

Carbs mentioned are per meal. Fridge up to 3 days or Freeze up to 3 months .

INGREDIENTS

600g raw chicken breast

Tbsp. garlic powder

Tbsp. chilli powder

Black pepper

30g cornflour

20g olive oil

Tbsp. garlic

Tsp. ginger

Bell pepper & spring onion

50ml light soy sauce

70ml hot sauce

Tbsp. tomato paste

15g honey

200g uncooked rice

FULL RECIPE NEXT PAGE

THE ZACK CHUG Cookbook

Scan me !!

METHOD

- Get 600g raw chicken breast and cut into thin slices.

- Season with tbsp garlic powder, tbsp chilli powder, black pepper and cornflour to make it crispy.

- Mix together & optional to coat using a seal ziplock bag.

- Cook on high heat on a pan for 10 -15 mins with 20g olive oil until golden and crunchy.

- Then set chicken aside and add tbsp garlic, tsp ginger, bell pepper and spring onion.

- Add 50ml light soy sauce, 70ml hot sauce, tbsp tomato paste, 15g honey and cooked chicken.

- Stir and simmer on low to medium heat until a sticky glaze forms.

- Meanwhile cook 200g of uncooked washed rice (will equal roughly 630g cooked rice).

- Add to meal prep containers.

THE
ZACK CHUG
Cookbook

218

CHICKEN PASTA

Calories 380   **Carbs** 40g   **Protein** 38g   **Fat** 11g

Carbs mentioned are per meal.

FULL RECIPE NEXT PAGE

INGREDIENTS

600g raw chicken breast

Tbsp. oregano

Tbsp. garlic powder

Tbsp. cumin & paprika

Tsp. olive oil

30g light butter

Tbsp. garlic

Chopped onion

200ml skimmed milk (or milk of choice)

60g low fat cream cheese

30g parmesan cheese

Black pepper and parsley

600g cooked pasta

THE ZACK CHUG Cookbook

Scan me !!

METHOD

- Take raw chicken breast and season it with oregano, garlic powder, cumin & paprika and tsp olive oil.

- Mix together and oven or air fry for 15-20@ 220°C until juicy and tender.

- Then on low to medium heat, add light butter, tbsp garlic, chopped onion, skimmed milk (or milk of choice), low fat cream cheese, parmesan cheese, black pepper and parsley.

- Add 600g cooked pasta.

- Stir together until rich and creamy.

- Finish with leftover sauce from the pan.

- Add equal portions of spaghetti and chicken to your meal prep containers.

THE
ZACK CHUG
Cookbook

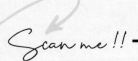

HIGH PROTEIN MEAL PREP RICH BUTTERY
GARLIC CHICKEN

Calories 350	**Carbs** 34g	**Protein** 32g	**Fat** 6g

Carbs mentioned are per meal.

INGREDIENTS

600g raw chicken breast

Tbsp. oregano

Tbsp. garlic powder

Tbsp. cumin & black pepper

Tbsp. paprika & olive oil

30g light butter

Tbsp. garlic

Tsp. tomato paste

20g honey

Chilli flakes & coriander

200g uncooked rice.

FULL RECIPE NEXT PAGE

THE ZACK CHUG Cookbook

Scan me !!

METHOD

- Dice 600g raw chicken breast and season with tbsp oregano, tbsp garlic powder, tbsp cumin, black pepper tbsp paprika and tbsp olive oil.

- Then on medium heat, add 30g light butter, tbsp garlic, tsp. tomato paste, seasoned raw chicken from before, honey, chilli flakes and coriander.

- Cool the chicken for 15 mins and let it simmer until sticky.

- Meanwhile, cook 200g uncooked washed rice (roughly will form 630g cooked rice).

- Add equal portions of rice and chicken to your meal prep containers.

THE
ZACK CHUG
Cookbook

FAQS

FAQS

• WHAT BLENDER DO YOU USE?

For blending into a mixture, I always use a Nutribullet blender.

• WHAT IS OAT FLOUR?

Oat flour is normal rolled oats blended up, if I use 30g of oats it'll form 30g oat flour.

• WHAT ARE THE ESSENTIAL ITEMS I SHOULD BUY ON MY GROCERY LIST FOR YOUR RECIPES?

Low fat Greek yoghurt, paprika, oregano & garlic seasoning, oats eggs, mozzarella cheese, unsweetened almond milk, baking powder cocoa powder, chicken breast, cocoa powder, vegetables of choice tortilla wraps, pasta/rice/potatoes, low cal oil spray.

• WHAT DO I MEAN BY COOKED CHICKEN BREAST?

This is raw chicken breast marinaded in paprika, pepper, salt, garlic, and oregano. I cook the chicken on a pan on medium heat for 10 minutes using low calorie oil spray.

• HOW MANY GRAMS IN ONE SCOOP OF PROTEIN POWDER?

32g.

• WHAT DO I MEAN BY PAN FRY?

Cooking your meat on a pan on medium to high heat, I oil my pan using low calorie oil spray.

• WHY DO SOME MACROS ON HERE DIFFER TO THE ONES IN YOUR VIDEOS?

I have updated certain recipes in using different measurements and quantities in order to improve them ever since filming them.

• WHAT IF I DON'T HAVE AN AIR-FRYER?

You can utilise an oven as replacement, the cooking times may differ depending on how powerful your oven is.

• DO I HAVE TO PAY FOR THE NEW RECIPES?

NO, this purchase is a 1-time payment.

• HOW DO I ACQUIRE THE NEW RECIPES?

An updated file will be emailed to everyone who has purchased the cookbook.

• HOW CAN I USE THESE RECIPES TO BULK?

The best way to use this recipe to bulk is by replacing the ingredient.

For example, unsweetened almond milk (30 calories per cup) can be replaced with whole milk(s) (150+ calories per cup.

Olive oil instead of 0 calorie oil spray, whole eggs instead of egg whites, traditional condiments instead of sugar-free condiments e.t.c.

• WHAT DOES TSP. & TBSP. MEAN?

Teaspoon and tablespoon measurements

Copyright © 2022 Zack Chug

All rights reserved. This book or any portion thereof may not be reproduced or used in any manner whatsoever without the express written permission of the author except for the use of brief quotations in a book review.

Cover illustration by Martha Cruttenden

www.zackchugcookbook.com